The Asian Literature Bibliography Series

GUIDE TO CHINESE PROSE

The Asian Literature Program
of the Asia Society

General Editor

Guide to

CHINESE PROSE

JORDAN D. PAPER

G. K. HALL & CO.
70 LINCOLN STREET, BOSTON, MASS.
1973

Library of Congress Cataloging in Publication Data

Paper, Jordan D
   Guide to Chinese prose.

   (The Asian literature bibliography series)
   Bibliography: p.
   1. Chinese literature—Bibliography. I. Title.
II. Series.
Z3108.L5P34   016.8951'8'08   72-14082
ISBN 0-8161-1103-0

Acknowledgment

The "Key to Chinese Pronunciation" is reprinted from
The Travels of Lao Ts'an, by Liu T'ieh-yün, translated
by Harold Shadick. Copyright 1952 by Cornell University.
Used by permission of Cornell University Press.

CONTENTS

FOREWORD

This annotated bibliography series on Asian literature was initiated in response to the needs of the nonspecialist. It is hoped that the summaries and evaluations to selected works available in translation together with the general introduction in each guide to the literature under examination will aid educators and students on both the secondary and college level as well as the general reader and those institutions who want to build up responsibly their collection of Asian writings. Although compiled for an audience completely unfamiliar with Asian literature, these guides are also intended to be reference works for students and scholars exploring a particular subject. In addition, they should benefit those in disciplines other than literature—Asian heritage studies, anthropology, history, philosophy, the social sciences—who wish to take advantage of translated literature as a rich source of material for their studies. Books that are not available in libraries may be ordered through the publishers or through such specialized bookstores as Paragon Book Gallery, New York, Hutchins Oriental Books, California, or The Cellar Book Shop, Michigan.

Naturally, each author has his own criteria for the way the material in his guide is selected, presented, and judged. However, the intent of the author has been to indicate clearly and honestly the range and artistic merit of all the titles annotated and thereby guide the reader to those specific works which will most satisfy his scholarly and aesthetic needs.

Arranged by topic and by chronology, each guide covers the translated literature from the earliest times to today, but none pretend to be comprehensive. In most cases, works that are not recommended or have been superseded by better versions have been excluded. Omitted also are very specialized studies and inaccessible translations (thus excluding much of what has appeared in magazines and journals), and a number of translations which are too new to have been included in the guides. This increase in translation activities is a welcome sign. It points to a growing awareness of the importance of listening to Asian voices (rather than only to Western interpreters of Asia) and to the growing recognition of the place of Asian writings in world literature and of the place of translators in the creative field. Hopefully, these guides will serve the reader who later turns to translations not annotated or discussed here.

A series of this scope required the involvement of a number of people. I would especially like to thank the authors who have prepared these guides and the many scholars who have acted as consultants throughout the preparation of each manuscript, offering invaluable suggestions and criticism. Acknowledgment is also due Junnko Tozaki Haverlick of the Asian Literature Program of The Asia Society under whose editorial guidance these guides were prepared.

BONNIE R. CROWN, Director
The Asia Society   *Asian Literature Program*

Key to Chinese Pronunciation

Most Chinese "words" or names consist of from one to three syllables. The generally accepted system of transliterating Chinese used in the English-speaking world is the Wade-Giles system. Most of the syllables are represented in this sytem as consisting of two parts, an initial consonant and a final vowel or vowel group (sometimes ending in *n* or *ng*). Ten finals (*a, ai, an, ang, ao, e* or *o, en, ou, i, erh*) can form syllables without initials. The following tables show approximately how the Wade-Giles symbols should be pronounced.

INITIALS

Wade-Giles Symbol	Pronounced	Wade-Giles Symbol	Pronounced
ch	j in jay	p'	p in spill
ch'	ch in charm	s	s
f	f	sh	sh
h	h (slightly guttural)	ss or sz (only used before u)	s
hs	sh	t	d
j	r	t'	t
k	g in gay	ts	dz
k'	k in skill	ts'	ts
l	l	tz (only before u)	dz
m	m	tz' (only before u)	ts
n	n	w	w in way
p	b in bait	y	y in you

FINALS

Wade-Giles Symbol	Pronounced	Wade-Giles Symbol	Pronounced
a	ah	ia	yah
ai	eye	iang	yahng
an	on in yon, or ann in mann (German)	iao	yow (ow in how)
ang	in lang (German)	ieh	yeah
		ien	yen
ao	ow in how	ih	rr (not trilled)
e or ê	u in cup		
ei	ay in say	in	in
en or ên	un in bun	ing	ing

3

Wade-Giles Symbol	Pronounced	Wade-Giles Symbol	Pronounced
eng or êng	ung in bung	iu	ew in mew
		iung	ee + ung, or
erh or êrh	er in ermine		jung (German)
i (sometimes written yi when there is no other initial)	ee	o (after initials other than h and k)	aw in law
o (after h and k or without initial)	u in cup	uang	oo + ang in lang (German)
		ui (wei)	way
ou (ow)	ow in low	un	un in und (German)
u (after initials other than ss or sz, tz, tz')	oo	ung	ung in bung (German)
u or ŭ or e (after ss or sz, tz, tz')	indicates prolonged buzz produced by voicing the consonant	uo	uaw in squaw
		ü	ü in über (German)
		üan	ü + ann in mann, (German)
		üeh (io)	ü + eah in yeah, or ue in luette (French)
ua	wa in wand, or ua in guava		
uai	wi in wine	ün	une (French)
uan	wan, or uan in Don Juan (Spanish)		

A FEW EXAMPLES OF COMPLETE SYLLABLES

Wade-Giles	Components	Complete Syllable as in
so	s + o	saw
lao	l + ao	(al)low
tao	t + ao	Dow
t'eng	t' + eng	tongue
T'ieh	t + ieh	(twen)ty hei(rs)
Liu	l + iu	(loca)l u(nion) or lieu
Ts'an	ts' + an	(i)t's Hon(duras)
ying	y + ing	(pla)ying
yün	y + ün	(cit)y un(ion)

Chronological Table

DYNASTIES

Shang			?–1027 B.C.
Chou			1027– 221 B.C.
	Western Chou	1027–771	
	Eastern Chou	770–249	
	Ch'un-ch'iu		
	(Spring and Autumn)	722–481	
	Chan-kuo (Warring States)	403–221	
Ch'in			221–206 B.C.
Han			202 B.C.–A.D. 220
	Former Han	202 B.C.–A.D. 8	
	Hsin	A.D. 8–23	
	Later Han	25–220	
Six Dynasties			220–589
	San-kuo (Three Kingdoms)	220–265	
	Western Chin	265–317	
	Northern and Southern		
	Dynasties	317–589	
Sui			589–618
T'ang			618–907
Five Dynasties			907–960
Sung			960–1279
	Northern Sung	960–1126	
	Southern Sung	1127–1279	
Yüan			1260–1368
Ming			1368–1644
Ch'ing			1644–1912

TWENTIETH CENTURY

1911	Republic proclaimed
1917	Hu Shih begins literary revolution
1919	May 4th Movement
1921	Chinese Communist Party founded
1931	Japanese expand into Manchuria
1937	Japanese occupy coastal China and Yangtze valley
1945	End of Second World War
1949	Founding of People's Republic of China; Nationalist government withdraws to Taiwan.

5

INTRODUCTION

Traditional Chinese bibliographic classification divides literature into four classes: Classics, history, philosophy and belles
lettres. The latter would include essays, poetry, and fiction.
Most fiction in the vernacular, including the novel, was not
considered literature and was, hence, unclassified. This bibliography will cover all genres of Chinese literature except poetry
and drama, which developed within the tradition of poetry.

The Chinese Language

Chinese is the only language of the world's contemporary
major civilizations except Japanese that developed independent
of the Indo-European language family (which includes Sanskrit
and most European languages); and Chinese, as a written language, is radically different from all other major languages. To
fully appreciate Chinese literature in translation, it is necessary
to have some understanding of the language.

An outstanding feature of written Chinese is that it is not
directly related to the spoken language; where the written symbols of Indo-European and other languages represent spoken
sounds, so that their writing is in essence a code for the spoken
language, the written symbols of Chinese represent concepts.
Although spoken Chinese, like all living languages, changed
over time, the written language, as it was not grounded on
the spoken, did not necessarily change with the spoken. Thus,
there developed in China two distinct types of language: the
spoken, which altered in time and area so that there developed
numerous dialects, some of which are almost separate tongues;
and the written, which in its literary or classical form, remained
relatively constant. The temporal constancy of the written language in part accounts for the Chinese cultural emphasis on
history; until the present century, an educated Chinese could
read books in his language written nearly three thousand years
ago. The geographical constancy of the language partially
accounts for the relative unity and stability of Chinese

civilization; an educated Chinese could communicate in writing, if not in speech, anywhere in China.

The earliest Chinese written symbols can be found on documents written approximately 1500 B.C. These symbols are directly related to ones in current use and a number can be read with their current literary meanings. It is clear that the earliest were pictographic: e.g., ⊙ stood for the sun and ☽ for the moon. But there are many concepts which cannot be expressed pictographically and ideographs were formed: ⊙☽, a combination of the sun and moon, means bright, extended later to mean intelligent as well. As the language grew, linguistic compounds were formed. Meanings from spoken words were either added to already existing symbols with the same sound but a different meaning, or new compounds were formed, combining an element signifying the sound and another signifying part of the meaning. In the developed form of the language, most symbols or characters are linguistic compounds and proportionally few are pictographs.

The characters, which can have a number of meanings, sometimes unrelated, and different pronunciations depending on meaning, are usually arranged in subject-verb-object word order. The function of the characters, many of which can serve as noun, verb, or modifier, is dependent upon their place in the word order. As literary Chinese was not punctuated, here was an added potential for confusion. Written Chinese is terse, compact, and contains extensive literary and historical allusions. The beauty of the language derives in large part from the taut construction which, to the translator, however, causes tremendous difficulties. Vernacular fiction and most prose written since the Literary Revolution of this century approximate the spoken language and are immune to many translation problems, but are lacking in esthetic qualities.

Literature in Chinese Culture

One of the remarkable characteristics of Chinese culture is its emphasis on literature—the written word was a predominant aspect of the civilization. By 500 B.C., writing instruments were a standard feature of the equipage of the aristocrats. China pioneered in the development of writing materials, including paper and "India" ink, as well as inventing printing, in the search for better and more inexpensive means of producing books. Under the influence of Confucianism the written word was imbued with spiritual qualities and it was improper to treat written material callously. Even before the historical period, writing was the means for communicating with the spirits.

Following the complete establishment of the "Civil Service" system by A.D. 1000, the primary means of gaining wealth and fame, of entering the upper classes, was through education. Proficiency in writing essays and skill in calligraphy were essential to the civil service examinations. Important government officials were noted not only for their administrative excellence and scholarship, but also for their compositions in prose and poetry and skill in the arts. It is generally accepted that by about 1750, more books had been published in China than in all the rest of the world.

The History of Chinese Prose: Early Period

In the earliest Chinese writing found to date, on the "oracle bones" of the Shang period (?–1027 B.C.) (no. **16**), Chinese is already a developed language. These writings are not literature *per se*, but questions put to the ancestors of the king with responses and sometimes results of divinations. Aside from the texts cast into the bronze vessels, there are several literary remains from the Early or Western Chou period. Chou, an agricultural semi-vassal state to the northwest of Shang, conquered its overlords after a thoroughly planned invasion in 1027 B.C. Among the earliest Chinese documents are the speeches of the Chou prime minister to the conquered Shang aristocrats.

The earliest works were formed into a corpus entitled the Five Classics (no. **26**) in the Han dynasty. Originally there were six Classics, but the *Classic of Music* was lost at an early date. The Classics comprise the *I ching* (Book of Changes, no. **27**), *Shu ching* (Book of Documents, no. **29**), *Shih ching* (Book of Odes), *Ch'un ch'iu* (Spring and Autumn Annals, no. **30**), and the *Li ching*, books on ritual considered as a single unit (the *Li chi* (no. **31**), *I li* and *Chou li* are the three primary works).

The basic portion of the *I ching*, a divination manual, may even predate the Chou conquest; some documents within the authentic part of the *Shu ching*, a collection of historical documents, immediately antedate the Chou conquest. The *Shih ching*, a collection of folk and court songs, and the *Ch'un ch'iu*, an extremely terse chronological history of one of the Chou states, are of the middle Chou period. Although containing earlier material, the books on ritual were composed toward the end of the Chou period and into the Han.

Aside from the Classics, there is a single work which may contain elements as early as the Shang period, but much research has yet to be done on the *Shang hai ching* (Book of Mountains and Seas), a fantastic geography not yet translated into English. Two historical works, the *Tso chuan* (no. **30**) and the *Kuo yü* (Conversations of the States, untranslated) date to the mid-Chou period, and a third, the *Chan-kuo ts'e* (Intrigues of the Warring States, nos. **33, 34)** provides the name for the period it covers— 403–221 B.C. These histories include the earliest narrative prose and fiction.

Most of the extant literary works of the Chou period are philosophical, although the Chinese use of the term is broader than the Western. The Warring States period was one of the greatest periods of intellectual ferment in Chinese history. The unity of Chou feudalism had long since collapsed and the now independent states were each striving to conquer the others; the civilization was in the midst of massive social and cultural change.

After Confucius (551–479 B.C.) broke with tradition and became the first professional teacher, there was, in the Warring States period, a proliferation of philosophical schools and teachers. Princes avidly sought after these teachers, each prince looking for a way to unify China under his own individual authority. Ssu-ma Ch'ien, a historian of the second century B.C., speaks of the "Hundred Schools" which encompassed cosmology, divination, logic, military science, administration, agriculture, and medicine, as well as political and ethical philosophy.

Among the most important thinkers are, in chronological order, Confucius (no. **47**), Chuang-tzu (nos. **60, 61**), Mo-tzu (nos. **52–54**), Mencius (nos. **49–51**), Hsün-tzu (nos. **52, 55–57**),

Lao-tzu (nos. **63–66**), and Han Fei-tzu (nos. **52, 58, 59**). Their works are of interest not only for their philosophical content but also for their literary relevance. Here are the earliest developed prose styles: essays, logical arguments, and dialogues.

The first part of the *Chuang-tzu* contains the oldest and most important Taoist writings, but the *Tao te ching,* a collection of enigmatic statements, has become more widely known in the West. The school of Mo-tzu is the only one of these mentioned which did not survive as a viable philosophy after the Chou period. Mencius and Hsün-tzu were the most important proponents of the doctrines of Confucius. Han Fei-tzu was the primary Legalist thinker.

Aside from those translation difficulties due to the nature of literary Chinese previously discussed, there are further problems in reading these early works. With very early texts such as the *I ching* and *Shu ching,* early meanings of characters and grammatical usages may have been lost and later interpretations inadvertently substituted. The *Chuang-tzu* is from a southern tradition of which there are few literary remains; grammar and vocabulary differ from the mainstream of Chinese literature and the work contains terms that are only found in this one book. The early books were composed of vertical wooden and bamboo slips tied together with thongs (hence the custom of writing Chinese vertically) and rolled up. If the leather or silk cords were damaged, the order of the slips might easily have become confused. Books lost during the chaos of the Warring States period and the book-burnings of the following Ch'in dynasty were later reconstructed when possible. Other sources of error include copyists' mistakes, footnotes incorporated into the text, and deliberate additions.

The History of Chinese Prose: Middle Period

From the standpoint of literature, the short-lived Ch'in dynasty (221–206 B.C.) which succeeded in unifying China and founding the first Chinese empire, is noted for its infamous burning of books. The Ch'in emperor sought to destroy all literature, except for works on divination, agriculture, and medicine, in order to completely stifle dissent in his rigid totalitarian state. The Han dynasty (202 B.C.–A.D. 220) which followed the Ch'in was a powerful, expansionist period that saw the rapid extension of China's borders and civilization. It compares favorably with the Roman Empire with which it was contemporaneous. The Han dynasty was a period of synthesis and consolidation rather than of creativity. Many of the diverse philosophies of the Chou period were assimilated into the Confucian and Taoist traditions, and these two traditions partly merged in the century following the Han dynasty.

Because the first Han emperors maintained the totalitarian government of the Ch'in, although in not as harsh a fashion, they were criticized by the Confucians. To eradicate this criticism of the government's policies, their energies were turned toward literary activities. The emperors sponsored literary studies and attempts to reconstruct books destroyed by the Ch'in and also established a large university oriented toward literary research.

Eventually this support led to the development of the civil service system, in which government officials were chosen through a series of highly competitive examinations based on ethical interpretations of the Classics. The government became Confucian in that scholars now were chosen for the top administrative posts; but, as the scholars were totally under the control of the emperor, and the civil service examination system was a means of regulating the officials, the government continued its totalitarian tone. The degree of the emperor's control varied from period to period but was especially strong from the fifteenth through the nineteenth centuries.

In the Han dynasty, many literary aids were compiled, including the fixing of the texts of the "Confucian" Classics, the first bibliographical studies, and the first etymological dictionary. Perhaps the most important literary developments were in historiography. Some historians consider the two greatest contributions of Chinese civilization to be methods of government administration and historiography. Ssu-ma Ch'ien wrote a massive work, the *Shih chi* (Historical Records, nos. **35, 37**), which covered the known world from its legendary beginnings to his own time. Pan Ku, modeling himself on the style of the *Shih chi,* wrote the *Han shu* (History of the Former Han Dynasty, no. **38**) which became the archetypal dynastic history. Following this model, each succeeding dynasty compiled a history of the preceding one—the major reason Chinese history is conceived of in terms of dynasties.

Following the Han dynasty, China suffered four centuries of relative political chaos. In the early fourth century, Central Asian nomads invaded the northern part of China and many Chinese, especially the educated, fled to the south, then newly under Chinese cultural domination. This mass migration had considerable effects on Chinese culture: in the North, a strong, "foreign," Buddhist "Caesero-papist" state prevailed; while in the South, because of the concentration of the educated and the freedom from tradition in a frontier area, a civilization with an intense, highly original intellectual life thrived.

In the third century A.D., Taoism and Confucianism combined to form a school of philosophy called *hsüan-hsüeh* (lit., "subtle learning," usually translated "Neo-Taoism"; nos. **22, 25, 45**), which incorporated the institution of *ch'ing-t'an* ("Pure Discourse"), a social as well as philosophical mode of discourse emphasizing wit and humor. A compilation of the best of these conversations was made in the fifth century, entitled *Shih shuo hsin yü* (New Specimens of Contemporary Talk), of which a complete scholarly English translation is expected within a few years. The *Lieh-tzu* (no. **67**) is a fascinating Taoist work of this time incorporating earlier material.

Buddhism, which had been introduced into China sometime during the Former Han dynasty, became dominant in Chinese life and thought during the chaotic Six Dynasties period (A.D. 220–589). The introduction of Buddhism led to the development of methods of transliteration, increasingly vast translation activities, and increased knowledge of non-Chinese cultures.

In the Six Dynasties period, scholars began to collect *chih-kuai* ("tales of the supernatural," no. **84**). These were not original fiction, but stories recorded in a journalistic fashion. A number of these collections incorporated stories of Buddhist and Indian origin. Fiction was considered of slight literary merit and called *hsiao-shuo* (lit., "small talk").

The earliest form of colloquial fiction also dates from the close of this period. There appeared a type of prose narrative utilizing poetic bridges called *pien-wen*, the predecessor of the professional storyteller's tales of the Sung dynasty. The subjects were both secular and religious, the latter stories told by peripatetic Buddhist monks who alternated verse or passages from the *sutras* ("scripture") with illustrative stories, on, for example, the lives of the Buddha (no. **85**).

Further literary developments in the Six Dynasties period include the beginning of literary criticism (no. **74**) and *p'ien-wen* ("Parallel Prose") which originated in the Han style of prose-poetry called *fu* (see *Guide to Chinese Poetry* in this series). Toward the end of this period, a distinction came to be made between belles lettres and utilitarian prose. Parallel Prose is an elegant, artifical form of prose usually based on four- and six-character phrases parallel in verbal and grammatical structure; i.e., prose written with poetic devices. Although the esthetic aspects are usually untranslatable, examples will be found in the "Anthologies" section of this bibliography.

The short-lived Sui dynasty (589–618) reunited China and was followed by the T'ang (618–907), a strong, cosmopolitan era. In the early part of the T'ang dynasty, the emperors maintained a close relationship with Buddhism, continuing the Northern, "Caesero-papist" style. Chinese Buddhism matured in this period, especially following the journey of the monk Hsüan-tsang to India (nos.**41, 42**) and the translation activities on his return.

The *Yu hsien k'u* (Journey to the Abode of the Fairies, no. **86**) is the earliest known consciously created short story written in the literary style (although the introductions to Han dynasty *fu* might be considered earlier examples). Based on an early romantic theme, the tale utilizes an ornate prose style as the connecting narrative between the larger amounts of poetry recited by the protagonists.

The History of Chinese Prose: Early Modern Period

Many historians now trace the beginning of China's modern or early modern period to the eighth century or mid-T'ang dynasty. From this time on, one can see the development of a new civilization quite different in tone and mood from the preceding era that continued without major changes into the nineteenth century. There was a transition from a martial to a pacifist orientation; from a cosmopolitan to a narrower, more ethnocentric view; from a per capita tax to one on land which enabled the rapid growth of commercial activities, a change to a complete monetary economy, and the development of banking institutions. Furthermore, the examination system became fully developed, with a corresponding change in society from an aristocracy based on land, to a more fluid, egalitarian structure based on moral and intellectual superiority. The geographical and cultural center of China shifted to the south a few centuries later, and within a hundred years, Buddhism was suppressed with permanent results. Only the Chinese variants such as *Ch'an* ("Zen", nos. **68, 69**) survived, and Neo-Confucianism within several centuries replaced Buddhist dominance.

Following the collapse of the T'ang, there was a short period of political instability, the Five Dynasties and Ten Kingdoms period (907–960). Thereafter, Chinese civilization became so stable that one dynasty would replace another with but slight breaks in governmental authority. The Sung dynasty (960–1279) lost the north to a non-Chinese people in 1126, resulting in the second mass migration to the south, and all China was lost to the Mongols by 1279. The Sung, especially the Southern Sung, was nearly opposite in spirit to the T'ang. Chinese culture underwent an intensification, a rapid development never surpassed in Chinese history. In the arts, the period is noted for great strides in painting, ceramics, architecture, and gardening.

The most important literary development in the late T'ang period was the *ku-wen* ("Ancient Style") movement. Led by Han Yü, the movement sought to replace the Parallel Prose style which was of limited usefulness with a return to Han dynasty models. *Ku-wen,* because it sought its models in antiquity, maintained the artificiality of the literary language but, unlike Parallel Prose, was suited to narrative writing. The *ku-wen* movement was only part of a larger cultural and political movement that strove to end the influence of Buddhism and other foreign innovations by stressing the Classics in the civil service examinations and returning to Confucian ethics with its emphasis on filial piety. Initially successful, the proponents of *ku-wen* did not completely replace the use of Parallel Prose until the Sung dynasty, when a number of superb essayists like Wang An-shih (no. **73**) insured *ku-wen* of its dominance in Chinese prose until the twentieth century.

The rise of *ku-wen* led to a new style of fiction in the late T'ang, *ch'uan-ch'i* ("tales of the marvelous"). Although many of the subjects came from earlier recorded *chih-kuai* tales, *ch'uan-ch'i* (nos. **86, 87**) was the earliest of consciously created Chinese fiction. The themes of these tales were usually the marvelous, heroic, religious, and love.

From *pien-wen*, fiction in the vernacular reached a second stage of development in the Sung dynasty. By this time, we know that professional storytellers were so numerous that they had their own guilds. The widespread use of printing led to the publication of storytellers' promptbooks *(hua-pen)*. Scholars began to write these promptbooks as an avocation, and they became the inspiration for the later writing of colloquial short stories, drama, and novels.

Great strides in scholarly writings also characterized the Sung dynasty. A number of encyclopedias on various subjects were produced and developments in historiography include the great universal history of Ssu-ma Kuang (no. **39**).

In 1260, the Mongols founded the Yüan dynasty, which lasted but a century. Due to the increased use of the vernacular by the less highly educated Mongols and the refusal of many of the Chinese scholars to hold office under them, novels and drama began to be written in the vernacular (*pai-hua:* "plain or unadorned speech") by the self-retired officials. These novels and drama, based on the historical and romantic episodes strung together in the promptbooks, were called *p'ing hua* in the Yüan dynasty. The earliest novels, though not their final forms, date from this time: *Romance of the Three Kingdoms* (no. **98**), *Water Margin* (nos. **99, 100**) and *Journey to the West* (no. **103**).

A native dynasty replaced the Mongols in 1368. The Ming emperors were more despotic and sought a tighter control of the scholar-officials than had the Sung. They continued the Yüan modification of the civil service examinations, basing them on a single orthodox interpretation of the Classics, that of the great Sung Neo-Confucian philosopher, Chu Hsi. A second development was the adoption of a formal, rigid style for writing the examinations, the "eight-legged essay." These two developments tended to stifle creative thought and, over a long period of time, to weaken Chinese government and culture.

The Manchus conquered China, ending the rule of the decaying Ming dynasty, and began the Ch'ing in 1644. In the first century of Ch'ing rule, China was the most powerful nation in the world; but by the nineteenth century, in confrontation with the rapidly expanding West, China was so weak as to be easily humiliated.

Prose developments during the Ming and Ch'ing dynasties include the growth of the novel and its maturity in the eighteenth century with the *Dream of the Red Chamber* (nos. **111, 112**), China's greatest novel, and *The Scholars* (no.**115**), a novel of social criticism. A strong interest in eroticism existed during the last century of Ming rule, centering in the city of Nanking. Two novels evidence this phenomena: *Chin P'ing Mei* (nos. **106, 107**) and *Jou p'u t'uan* (no. **110**). This phase of Chinese literature ended with the Ch'ing dynasty's emphasis on literary censorship and puritanical morality. Short stories, both in the literary language, with the writings of P'u Sung-ling (nos. **89, 90**), and in the vernacular, especially with the writings of Feng Menglung (nos. **93, 94**), reached maturity in this period. Feng Menglung's stories were basically *ch'uan-ch'i* rewritten in *pai-hua* from literary Chinese.

The History of Chinese Prose: Twentieth Century

Nineteenth-century China was in a state of rapid decline due both to internal decay and external attack by the West and Japan. A number of reform movements of various types failed. In 1912, the Ch'ing dynasty was overthrown, but political instability continued for nearly another four decades. Attempts at parliamentary government and return to dynastic rule failed; power became concentrated in the hands of local warlords. An increasingly serious conflict developed between the Kuomintang (Nationalist Party) led by Chiang K'ai-shek and the Chinese Communist Party under the leadership of Mao Tse-tung. Following the defeat of the Japanese at the end of the Second World War and the failure of an attempted coalition government between the two, the Communists rapidly consolidated their control over China while the Kuomintang and its army were forced into exile on Taiwan, an island that had been under Japanese rule and culture for fifty years until it was ceded to China by the Allies at the end of the war.

Due to the transformation of Chinese civilization, literary developments in twentieth-century China are so different from past tradition that they properly belong in a separate study. Most Chinese literature, no matter what genre or period, was more or less didactic, but, whereas pre-twentieth-century literature had been in the main concerned with ethics, recent Chinese literature seeks to inculcate a revolutionary spirit and arouse feelings of reform and patriotism.

Previously, Chinese literature had been directed toward an educated elite. Keeping to traditional styles, the written language had been separated from the spoken for over a millenium. Those forms of fiction written in a style approximating the vernacular had no literary status. To intellectuals in the early twentieth century, it became increasingly clear that their civilization was in immediate need of massive reform. Stimulated by knowledge of the West, including European literature, Hu Shih and others began in 1917 to urge the general use of *pai-hua* ("vernacular") as opposed to *ku-wen-yen* ("literary language"). Some even advocated the use of romanization in place of Chinese characters. (This written form was tried again in the late 1940s, but is unsuited to Chinese and leads to considerable confusion.) The effects of the "May Fourth Movement" of 1919 (no. **125**) insured the success of the *pai-hua* movement and mobilized intellectuals and students into active political involvement. In 1920, the Ministry of Education ordered the teaching of *pai-hua* in the elementary schools. As it radically simplified written Chinese, this considerably increased the literacy of the population. Most of the literate, however, were then cut off from their literary past.

Except as a medium for fiction, writers had had no experience with *pai-hua*, but desire to communicate with the masses led to its increased and, at first, often awkward use. Abandoning traditional forms, writers began to search for a new style based in part on Western models. Most intellectuals, due to conviction or circumstances, inclined toward the leftist political position. The earliest successful author in the new style was Lu Hsün (nos. **133, 134**), who has become the father of modern Chinese literature.

In the 1930s, several writers came to the fore, including Mao Tun (nos. **135, 136**), Lao She (nos. **137, 138**) and Pa Chin (no. **139**). Because most Chinese authors of this period were primarily interested in the revolutionary effect of their work, Western readers living in different circumstances may find difficulty in appreciating their writings. However, the best works continue to embody the typical humaneness of traditional Chinese fiction and thus have universal appeal. Of the novels, Lao She's *Camel Hsiang-tzu* (no. **137**) is especially recommended and, of the short stories, Mao Tun's *Spring Silkworms* (no. **136**).

Chinese authors of the early forties were fundamentally concerned with and involved in the struggle against Japan. Following the success of the Communist Party, writers have been restricted both in the People's Republic and Taiwan. Compulsion to submit to political orthodoxy and thought reform has severely restricted the originality and scope of Communist authors. On Taiwan, the enforced official attitude is that most twentieth-century authors, being leftist, are treasonous; the necessity for authors to follow a narrow political line has had similar results. *Changes in Li Village* by Chao Shu-li (no. **141**) is an example of one of the better Communist works.

Entries and Annotations

Although a major portion of the world's literature is Chinese, only a relatively small amount has been translated into English, and only a small part of this competently. The reason lies in the unusual translation difficulties and the limited contact between the respective civilizations. Still, nearly all of China's greatest and most important literature has been translated, several works numerous times out of proportion to their value. English translation activities were pioneered by the British, led by such scholars as James Legge, Herbert Giles and Arthur Waley, the latter also an important translator of Japanese literature. In other European languages, the French have been even more notable in producing early excellent translations. Since 1949, in part due to the American preoccupation with Communism and the resultant government and foundation support of Chinese studies, a large number of often excellent works has been published in the United States.

The entries selected for annotation are divided into major categories according to traditional Chinese bibliographical classification discussed at the beginning of this introduction. Within each major category or subsection, the works are usually arranged chronologically. In the section on history, however, travel and biographies not in the standard histories are placed at the end of the section.

The "General Studies" category, the first in the bibliography, includes introductory and general works of a diverse nature that cover more than one type of Chinese literature. Within each category, introductory works and studies in that particular aspect of Chinese literature are placed before the translations, except for those studies which are specific to one particular work. These are placed immediately following the relevant work. The "Anthologies" category encompasses those works which again cover more than one type of literature; more specific anthologies will be found within the various sections.

All of the Classics are annotated except for the one on poetry and the ones on ritual; the latter are of little interest to the general reader, and the former will be covered in the *Guide to Chinese Poetry* of this series. Only the most important translated histories are annotated. Except for the very early works, none are available in their entirety. A number of philosophical works are entered, not only because many have been translated into English, but because these are the most important and numerous of the writings from the early period of Chinese prose. Most of the philosophical entries are of the early formative period. Except for two *Ch'an* ("Zen") works, later works, including important Chinese Buddhist and influential Neo-Confucian writings, were not annotated, as understanding of these writings requires a background in Buddhist or Chinese philosophy. Selections from these works can be found in the anthologies.

The section "Belles Lettres" has been arbitrarily arranged. The emphasis on fiction reflects the large number of translations available, not the value placed on this type of literature by the Chinese. "Further Readings Unannotated" is a select group of works either of a reference nature or complementary to the annotated selections; it should by no means be considered a complete list.

The annotations were written for readers with limited background knowledge of Chinese literature, but the needs of beginning students have also been considered. Evaluations made with the general reader in mind may at times conflict with the interests of the specialist. For example, a well-written, sometimes inaccurate translation may be preferable in this context to a superior, scholarly translation that is not nearly as readable or that assumes prior knowledge.

The annotations are arranged sequentially and, if read in order, will provide supplementary material to the previous outline of the history of Chinese prose. To avoid repetition, entries that are directly related are annotated together.

Chinese names are rendered in their Chinese order—the family name first, followed by the personal name. Commas, dividing last and first names, have been used only where there might be cause for confusion. Cross-reference numbers in parentheses refer to entry numbers, not page numbers, unless otherwise indicated.

I am indebted to a number of scholars too numerous to mention, but the opinions expressed in this bibliography are solely my own and do not reflect those of the Asia Society or other authors in this series. My own personal preferences are not always reflected in this bibliography as the entries were selected according to their suitability and value for the general reader. Negative reviews are generally avoided save for those few works which have gained wide acceptance far beyond their merit.

ANNOTATED
BIBLIOGRAPHY

General Studies

1. Fitzgerald, C. P. *China: A Short Cultural History*. 3d ed., rev. Paperbound. New York: Frederich A. Praeger, 1961. xviii, 624 pp.
2. Reischauer, Edwin O., and Fairbank, John K. *East Asia: The Great Tradition*. A History of East Asian Civilization, vol. 1. Boston: Houghton Mifflin Co., 1960; London: George Allen & Unwin, 1961. xvii, 739 pp.
3. Li, Dun J. *The Ageless Chinese: A History*. 2d ed., rev. Paperbound. New York: Charles Scribner's Sons, 1971. xvi 586 pp.
4. Goodrich, L. Carrington. *A Short History of the Chinese People*. 3d ed., rev. New York: Harper & Brothers, 1959. xvii, 295 pp. (Paperback, Harper Torchbooks).

A basic knowledge of Chinese history is indispensable for an understanding of the development of Chinese literature or for the full understanding of any individual literary work. A number of good histories of China are available; these four are far from being an inclusive listing, but each is of value for different reasons.

The work by C. P. Fitzgerald is especially relevant as it emphasizes cultural developments. Three of the thirty chapters are directly concerned with literature. It is an excellent one-volume presentation covering Chinese history through the Ch'ing dynasty.

East Asia: The Great Tradition is undoubtedly the best introductory history available; it is reliable, incorporates the latest research to the time it was written, and is clear and unusually readable. Divided into three parts—China, Korea and Japan—it covers cultural and literary developments in each chronological period. Its sequel, *East Asia: The Modern Transformation* (Fairbank, Reischauer, and A. H. Craig, vol. 2, 1965), written in an entirely different format, does not include material on cultural developments, and is not divided into three separate sections, but treats East Asia as a unit.

Dun J. Li's history discusses Chinese civilization from its origins to 1963. The work is balanced, and cultural aspects are thoroughly covered. The author has been able to imbue the work with a sense of immediacy and understanding that is quite refreshing. Professor Li has also edited an excellent anthology of readings (no. 25) which, although not published as a companion volume, may easily be used as one.

L. Carrington Goodrich's standard, compact work hardly touches upon cultural and literary developments. However, it has no peer as a brief and reliable history of the development of Chinese civilization.

5. de Bary, William Theodore, and Embree, Ainslie T., eds. *A Guide to Oriental Classics*. New York: Columbia University Press, 1964. pp. 115–173. (Paperback).

A Guide to Oriental Classics is a select bibliography with brief annotations directed toward the needs of a teacher of an Asian humanities course. In the section on China, eighteen works of Chinese prose are covered—fourteen philosophical texts and four novels. Complete (and for some, selected) translations, secondary readings, and discussion topics are recommended for each work. Many of the books listed are discussed in this *Guide to Chinese Prose*, but a wider range of translations for each work will be found in the *Oriental Classics* guide.

6. Liu Wu-chi. *An Introduction to Chinese Literature*. Bloomington: Indiana University Press, 1966. 321 pp. (Paperback).

7. Kaltenmark, Odile. *Chinese Literature*. Tr. and expanded from the French version of 1948 by Anne-Marie Geoghegar. New York: Walker & Co., 1964. 146 pp. (Paperback).

8. Ch'en Shou-yi. *Chinese Literature: A Historical Introduction*. New York: Ronald Press Co., 1961. 665 pp.

9. Giles, Herbert. *A History of Chinese Literature*. (1901). Reprint with "A Supplement on the Modern Period" by Liu Wu-chi. New York: Frederick Ungar Publishing Co., 1967. ix, 510 pp.

10. Lai Ming. *A History of Chinese Literature*. New York: John Day Co., 1964, 439 pp. (Paperback, Capricorn Books).

Three full-length introductory studies of the history of Chinese literature have been produced in the past decade; unfortunately only one is satisfactory. Although negative reviews are normally avoided, inferior introductory works have gained wide acceptance and warrant annotation. Until the appearance of Liu Wu-chi's book, the work by Ch'en Shou-yi was better than no book at all, but it is far too large, detailed and confused for the general reader and too inaccurate and dependent on secondary material for the scholar. Lai Ming's work is hopelessly full of inaccuracies and oversimplifications; the romanization and wording are thoroughly confused and often incorrect.

In contrast, Liu Wu-chi's *An Introduction to Chinese Literature* is warmly recommended. Intended as an introductory work for the nonspecialist, it emphasizes the major developments and avoids superfluous detail, and the book is of manageable length and well organized. The book begins with an excellent essay on the characteristics of Chinese literature. Starting with the "dawn of Chinese language," the book is an informed and sensitive literary history. In dealing with the early period, Liu's stance tends to be more conservative (e.g., Confucius is the transmitter of the Classics), but these views are still widely maintained and are most respectable. The work is carried into modern times to approximately 1940. Notes are placed at the end of the book along with an extensive bibliography for further reading, a table of Chinese history, a glossary of Chinese words with the Chinese characters and page citations, and an index.

Herbert Giles's *A History of Chinese Literature,* recently reprinted, was for many decades the standard introductory work. The history incorporates large amounts of fine translations and summaries of the major Chinese literary works. However, a half century of extensive research has taken place since it was written so it is considerably out-of-date. For example, Giles writes that the author of the *Hung lou meng* (Dream of the Red Chamber) is unknown. The 1967 edition contains an excellent brief supplement on the modern period to 1950 by Liu Wu-chi, but the emphasis is on poetry and drama.

The slim volume by Odile Kaltenmark is an excellent summary of the history of Chinese literature, but because there is far more material than can be covered in its small format, the text is reduced to near-outline form with scarcely any explanatory material. The work could serve as a good introductory handbook.

11. Hightower, James Robert. *Topics in Chinese Literature: Outlines and Bibliographies.* Harvard-Yenching Institute Studies, vol. 3. rev. ed. Paperbound. Cambridge: Harvard University Press, 1962. 141 pp.

This is an excellent handbook to the study of Chinese literature. There are only sixty-two pages of actual text, but the material is remarkably compact and lucid. The work is divided into seventeen topics, each treated in a few pages, followed by a select but extensive bibliography of authorities and translations. Six of the topics are especially useful as an introduction to Chinese prose: "The Classics," "Early Expository Prose: The Philosophies," "Early Narrative Prose: History, Fiction, and Anecdote," "Fiction in the Literary Language," "Popular Language Fiction: The Tale and The Novel," and "The Literary Revolution."

12. Bishop, John L., ed. *Studies in Chinese Literature.* Harvard-Yenching Institute Studies, vol. 21. Paperbound. Cambridge: Harvard University Press, 1965. 247 pp.

This volume is a reprint of eight important studies of Chinese literature from the *Harvard Journal of Asiatic Studies.* Most of these articles are technical and require some background knowledge in order to be appreciated. However, an article by John L. Bishop, "Some Limitations of Chinese Fiction" (pp. 237–245), is invaluable for the general reader. He points out that in contrast to Western fiction, there are limitations of narrative convention and purpose in Chinese fiction; hence, the reader may more readily appreciate Chinese fiction in translation by understanding "what he must not expect of it." In discussing the development of these limitations, Bishop also indicates that realistic fiction in China and Europe has a number of features in common although they evolved differently.

13. Feng Yüan-chün. *A Short History of Classical Chinese*

Literature. Tr. by Yang Hsien-yi and Gladys Yang. China
Knowledge Series. Peking: Foreign Languages Press, 1958.
132 pp.

This work, part of the *China Knowledge Series,* deals with
Chinese literature from its beginnings to the May Fourth Movement of 1919 (see no. **122** for supplementary work covering
the period from that date to the past decade). The short history
is brief indeed; 112 small pages of actual text cover both poetry
and prose, about half of the material consisting of translated
excerpts from the literary works discussed. The works annotated
in this bibliography could not even be adequately covered
within so small a book. Yet, since this history was originally
written in Chinese, a number of works that have not been translated are discussed. For this reason, Feng's history is recommended only to those readers who are unable to read the more
complete literary histories listed.

14. Wang Chi-chen. "Traditional Literature: Nature and Limitations." In *China,* ed. by Harley Farnsworth MacNair. (1946).
   pp. 386–396. Berkeley: University of California Press, 1951.

At the outset of this interesting introductory article, Professor
Wang develops the thesis that the Chinese have no conception
of literature in the modern Western sense of the term; hence,
there is a basic obstacle to Western understanding of Chinese
traditional literature. While in the West the view of literature
is idealistic and thought of as "Art," in China, literature is
considered to be utilitarian; fiction *per se* does not have a place
in literature. This fundamental difference lies in the contrasting
development of literature in China and the West (as well as
in the vast dissimilarity in the development of the written languages and thought processes). "Failure to approach Chinese
literature historically has resulted in failure to understand the
true character of the writings of traditional literature and of
popular literature and to explain their shortcomings and weak-
nesses." Beginning with this thesis, Professor Wang presents
a brief but penetrating discussion of the history of Chinese
literature to the modern period.

15. Lu Hsün. *A Brief History of Chinese Fiction.* Tr. by Yang Hsien-yi and Gladys Yang. (1923). Peking: Foreign Languages Press, 1959. 462 pp.

Based on a series of lectures given between 1920 and 1924 at Peking University, this is the only available comprehensive work on Chinese fiction and provides an excellent, if slightly dated, introduction to a major aspect of Chinese literature. Lu Hsün, himself one of the most important authors of Chinese fiction in this century, presented this material in response to the May Fourth Movement of 1919. Included at the end of the volume is Lu Hsün's *Historical Development of Chinese Fiction,* a series of lectures delivered in 1924; in fifty pages it essentially summarizes the material preceding it.

The twenty-eight chapters cover the broad spectrum of Chinese fiction, from the earliest use of *hsiao-shuo* ("fiction") and early renderings of mythology, through its various developments to the evolution of the fully developed novels at the end of the Ch'ing dynasty. Each of the major novels is accorded a separate chapter, and these thirteen chapters may be used as an introductory handbook to the Chinese novel. Numerous translated excerpts from the originals are provided, and there are twenty-four plates reproducing woodcut illustrations and pages from early editions.

The translators have had considerable experience in translating Chinese fiction into English and their rendering is adequate. An extensive index with Chinese characters is provided, although the listing of titles in English translation, rather than in romanization, causes some confusion, since translations often vary.

16. Tsien Tsuen-hsuin. *Written on Bamboo and Silk: The Beginnings of Chinese Books and Inscriptions.* Chicago: University of Chicago Press, 1962. xiv, 233 pp.

"Written on bamboo and silk" is a Chinese expression for books and other writings from antiquity; bamboo, silk, and later, paper were the common writing materials used in China until about the sixth century A.D. In this fascinating account of the development of Chinese writing and books, Professor Tsien discusses records on bones and shells of Chinese antiquity, inscriptions on metal and clay, engravings on stone and jade, and early documents made of bamboo and wood. He also treats the use of silk as writing material, the development of paper and tools for writing, and the evolution of Chinese script. Chinese prose before and during the invention of printing is also examined. The work is well illustrated and contains a glossary, an extensive bibliography, and an index.

17. Watson, Burton. *Early Chinese Literature*. Paperbound. New York: Columbia University Press, 1962. 304 pp.

This volume, by an important and prolific translator of early Chinese literature, covers the period to approximately 100 A.D. It is divided into three sections: history, philosphy, and poetry. Each work of literature is considered separately, and these discussions can easily serve as individual introductions to translations. The section on history is especially good; the material, with translated illustrative passages, is treated primarily from the literary standpoint. The section on philosophy, although useful, combines discussions of the philosophical and literary aspects of the works, to the detriment of both. This work is highly recommended; it is knowledgeable, imaginative, very well written, and especially designed for the beginning student of Chinese literature.

18. Edwards, E. D. *Chinese Prose Literature of the T'ang Period, A.D. 618–906*. 2 vols. Probsthain's Oriental Series, vol. 23–24. London: Arthur Probsthain, 1937–1938. 236 and 433 pp.

E. D. Edwards's two-volume work on the prose literature of the T'ang dynasty (618–906 A.D.) is the most comprehensive study of the entire prose literature of any one period of Chinese history. The study is based on an analysis of and translations from the *T'ang tai ts'ung shu* (Collected Works of the T'ang Dynasty). Edwards was especially interested in studying the development of Chinese fiction, much of which took place during the T'ang dynasty, and the social life of this period. For these purposes, the *T'ang tai ts'ung shu* is most useful because it is a collection of 144 books, supposedly of the T'ang period, covering a multitude of subjects.

The first volume of Edwards's study covers everything except fiction, which is treated in the second volume. Following introductory material on Chinese prose, there are discussions of history, art, science, religion, drama, and individual discussions of the first eighty-five books in the collection, including sample translations.

Volume two contains an essay on the development of early Chinese fiction, and notes on, and extensive translations from, the second half of the *T'ang tai ts'ung shu*. Although a large number of the myths, love stories, heroic and supernatural tales are complete, some, by necessity, are presented in abbreviated form. Each translation is preceded by an informative introduction and contains explanatory notes. The translations are among the best to be found of Chinese fiction; they maintain in English to a remarkable degree the literary qualities of the originals.

Aside from being a collection of superior translations of Chinese prose, the work has been a major contribution to Western studies of Chinese literature. In addition to the abovementioned studies, notes on the authenticity of the works in the *T'ang tai ts'ung shu* and extensive indices are included. Characters are supplied in the text for all proper nouns.

Anthologies

19. Giles, Herbert A., ed. *Gems of Chinese Literature.* (1923, rev. and enlarged in 2 vols.). Paperbound in 1 vol. New York: Paragon and Dover Publications, 1965. xviii, 430 pp.

The prose selections (vol. 1 or pp. 1–286 of the paperback reprint) are arranged in chronological order, a format that is more useful than a topical one. The early, pre-Han dynasty selections are primarily very brief excerpts from philosophical and historical works. In this section the translations are obviously dated and deficient—they are paraphrased rather than translated, and the emphasis is on their use as aphorisms.

It is rather the selections from the Han dynasty to the twentieth century that determine the worth of the anthology. Giles has concentrated on belles lettres—essays, letters, proclamations, petitions to the emperors—a major genre of Chinese prose that is often neglected in collections of translations. For this reason, *Gems of Chinese Literature* is the best source for an understanding of the development of Chinese prose writing exclusive of philosophy, history, and fiction. "Against History," one of the few extant pieces by Ssu-ma Hsiang-ju (d. 117 B.C.); the famous letter by Li Ling (first century B.C.) to Su Wu; and an essay by Liu Ling, one of the "Seven Sages of the Bamboo Grove," on the joys of drunkenness are a few of the many selections Giles has included. All of the major prose stylists of the T'ang and Sung dynasties are represented and the translations from later periods include many works that are not found in other collections. Among these are an essay by Hsü Hsüeh (seventeenth century) on antiques and one by Yüan Mei (eighteenth century) on the art of dining.

As a foreword to the work, Giles provides introductory notes on the history of Chinese literature. The translations from each author are preceded by brief biographical notes; complete indices with the Chinese characters are at the end of the work.

20. Lin Yutang, ed. *The Wisdom of China and India.* New York: Random House, Modern Library, 1942. 1103 pp.

The second half of *The Wisdom of China and India* (pp. 565–1103) is relevant to this bibliography. This is divided into six sections, including one on poetry. The first, "Chinese Mysticism," contains a complete translation of the *Tao te ching* and a partial one of the *Chuang-tzu;* superior translations are available for each.

The second section, with the farfetched title, "Chinese Democracy," consists of selections from the *Documents of History, Mencius* (both translations by James Legge) and *Mo-tzu* (translated by Y.P. Mei). The first two are considered by Lin Yutang to be philosophies of democracy; however, although both do in fact contain the earliest statements similar to important aspects of contemporary Western government, such a use of the term "democracy" renders it meaningless. Mo-tzu is termed a religious teacher, which again considerably stretches the actuality. Nevertheless, the translations in this section are the standard ones. "The Middle Way," the third section, is comprised of reordered selections from the *Analects* of Confucius and the *Doctrine of the Mean.* (All of the above-mentioned works are discussed separately in this bibliography.)

It is only the last two sections that are recommended. "Sketches of Chinese Life" offers a good selection of short stories of various periods and the only complete translation, and a very fine one, of Shen Fu's *Six Chapters of a Floating Life* (no. **71**). The last section, "Chinese Wit and Wisdom," has excerpts from a number of works including the *Lieh-tzu,* and Lin Yutang's partial translation of Cheng Pan-ch'iao's *Family Letters of a Chinese Poet.* The latter is a rare intimate look into the thoughts of a compassionate scholar-official of the Ch'ing dynasty. It is easy to agree with Lin Yutang's statement that "the family letters of Cheng Pan-ch'iao and the *Six Chapters of a Floating Life* serve . . . better than anything else to show the kindly temper of the Chinese people and the typical spirit of the Chinese people, though not idealized, but as it was actually lived in China."

Lin Yutang provides introductory commentary expressing his own views at the beginning of each of the six sections and for each of the translations. There is no index.

21. Lin Yutang, ed. and tr. *The Importance of Understanding.*

Cleveland: World Publishing Co., 1960. 494 pp. (Paperback retitled *Translations from the Chinese*, Forum Books).

The contents are divided into fifteen topics such as "Love and Death," "After Tea and Wine," and "The Seasons." Within each there is no attempt at order. Lin Yutang writes in his preface, "there should be no order in a book of this kind which is designed for casual dipping." But the unfamiliar Western reader may well find himself confused when faced with a seemingly random selection of short pieces rapidly moving back and forth over twenty-five hundred years of literary history, especially when no real introductory material is provided.

The titles of the topics are sometimes misleading. The section entitled "Zen" contains brief excerpts from the *Lankāvatāra* and *Surangama Sutras*. Neither is of *Ch'an* (Japanese: "Zen") or even Chinese origin, although these Indian *sutras* are of importance in the development of Ch'an thought. There are further instances of carelessness: Lin Yutang generally uses his own modification of the Wade-Giles system of romanization, but there is, for example, no reason to use *Shan* for *Ch'an*.

Many interesting short pieces are found nowhere else in translation and thus the work is of value. The anthology is indeed suitable for "casual dipping," but the result may be a feeling of preciousness rather than of a real understanding of China or Chinese literature.

22. de Bary, W. T.; Chan, Wing-tsit; and Watson, Burton, comps. *Sources of Chinese Tradition*. New York: Columbia University Press, 1960. xxiv, 976 pp. (Paperback in 2 vols.).

This anthology, according to the compilers, "is meant to provide the general reader with an understanding of the background of Chinese civilization especially as this is reflected in intellectual and religious traditions which have survived into modern times." The book admirably fulfills this purpose, but the heavy concentration on selections from philosophical works does not present a true or balanced picture of Chinese civilization; the work could more accurately be titled "Sources of Chinese Intellectual History."

The work is well laid out and chronologically organized. Introductions to the chapters are of sufficient length to do justice to their subjects and each selection is further introduced, relating it to the other selections. Because of the excellence of these introductions, the work can be read alone without supplementary material. The translations, relatively recent at the time of publication, are by noted scholars and translators. The book provides a descriptive table of contents, map, chronological table, and index.

While this anthology is not oriented toward literature, it is a major source of selections from Chinese philosophical, and to a lesser extent, historical, writings. As is usual with anthologies of this type, it is also an important source for examples of Chinese essay writing; such prominent prose stylists as Han Yü, Ou-yang Hsiu, Wang An-shih, Su Shih and Ssu-ma Kuang are represented. There are also extensive selections from Chinese writings since the mid-nineteenth century.

23.   Birch, Cyril, ed. *Anthology of Chinese Literature: From Early Times to the Fourteenth Century.* New York: Grove Press, 1965. xxxiv, 492 pp. (Paperback).

One-third of the translations in this excellent anthology are from prose literature; the remainder consists of poetry and two plays. The majority of the pieces have been previously published, some in the works covered by this bibliography, but many can be found only in scattered journals not readily available. The versions selected are usually by recognized scholars and translators and form a superior collection. The prose translations are by Cyril Birch, J. I. Crump, A. C. Graham, J. R. Hightower, R. K. Rideout, Arthur Waley, and Burton Watson.

The prose works begin with excerpts from the early historical writings. These histories include the earliest Chinese narrative writing. The next prose group consists of discussions on the theme of death and includes three dialogues from the *Chuang-tzu*, and an edict of Emperor Wen and essay by Wang Ch'ung, both of the Han dynasty. Other writings from this period are five biographies from the historical writings of Ssu-ma Ch'ien.

From the Six Dynasties period, grouped under the heading "On Seclusion," are letters by Yang Yün and Hsi K'ang and T'ao Ch'ien's famous story, "Peach Blossom Spring." Also representing this period is an excerpt from Lu Chi's "Rhyme Prose on Literature," the first important work on literary criticism. Materials from the T'ang dynasty include six essays by Han Yü and one by Liu Tsung-yüan. Because of the inclusion of these essays, Birch's anthology is especially useful. Also from the T'ang dynasty are three short stories; the one by Yüan Chen is perhaps the most famous Chinese love tale. This story is later used in the drama, "Romance of the West Chamber."

The Sung dynasty is represented by a preface and essay by Ou-yang Hsiu and a long letter to the Emperor by Su Shih (Su T'ung-p'o), both master prose stylists. The prose piece from the Yüan dynasty consists of chapters 14–16 of the early novel, *Shui hu chuan*.

The anthology contains a general introduction and introductions to the selections that are too brief to be sufficient for an understanding of the material. Also there are no explanatory notes concerning literary and historical allusions, a serious omission. It is suggested that this anthology be used in conjunction with, and as a supplement to, an introductory work on the history of Chinese literature. A brief bibliography is included.

24.　Chai, Ch'u, and Chai, Winberg, eds. and trs. *A Treasury of Chinese Literature: A New Prose Anthology, Including Fiction and Drama*. New York: Appleton-Century-Crofts, 1965. viii, 484 pp.

This anthology, designed "to serve the layman as [an] introduction to classical and modern Chinese prose literature" as well as "to bring to the Occident a little of *shu-hsiang* (fragrance of books)," succeeds remarkably well. The volume is divided into three parts: "General Prose," "Fiction," and "Drama" (only the first two parts will be discussed).

The first chapter of Part I, "Early Prose," is divided into two sections. The first, "Historical Writings," contains selections from the *Shu ching, Tso chuan, Chan-kuo ts'e* and *Shih chi*. The passages translated were chosen to illustrate "the fact that early narrative prose in China was closely linked with historiography is a significant feature of Chinese literature." The four histories are discussed separately in this guide (nos. **29, 30, 33, 34, 35**).

The second section of the first chapter contains selections from the philosophical writings *Mo-tzu*, *Mencius*, *Chuang-tzu* and *Han Fei-tzu*, which were chosen according to the criteria of literary form, style, and interest rather than philosophical speculation. Again, these works will be treated individually in the "Philosophy" section.

The following three chapters in Part I, "Medieval Essays," "Classical Essays," and "Modern Essays," are of especial interest, for these translations bring together an important aspect of Chinese literature which is otherwise only available in widely separated works. The "Medieval Essays" includes "A Pleading Memorial" to the emperor by Li Mi (264–316); "Preface to the Orchid Pavillion," a preface to a collection of poetry by Wang Hsi-chih (321–379); "Homeward Bound I Go," a prose poem; "The Peach Blossom Fountain [Spring]," the most important piece of early Chinese fiction; and "The Biography of Mr. Five Willows," a short autobiographical excursion by T'ao Ch'ien (365–427).

The selections for the "Classical Essays" illustrate the *ku-wen* ("ancient prose") or neoclassical movement in Chinese literature, beginning in the eighth century and continuing into the twelfth. Selections are from the writings of four of the "Eight Great Masters" of the T'ang and Sung dynasties: Han Yü (768–824), the leader of the movement; Liu Tsung-yüan (773–819); Ou-yang Hsiu (1007–1072); and Su Shih (Su Tung-p'o, 1036–1101), including his famous "The Red Cliff." The "Modern Essays," all written between 1925 and 1933, include the writings of Lu Hsün (1881–1936), Hsü Chih-mo (1896–1931), and Chu Tzu-ch'ing (1898–1948).

Part II, dealing with fiction, begins with five *ch'uan-ch'i* stories from the T'ang dynasty (see introduction p. 16). The chapter following contains two Sung dynasty *hua-pen* stories (see introduction p. 16). The combination of verse and story in the *hua-pen* illustrates the origin of colloquial fiction in the storyteller's presentation, but usually the verse sections are omitted in translation; in this work they are included. The third fiction chapter contains three stories from the *Liao-chai chih-i* by P'u Sung-ling (1640–1715) (nos. **89, 90**). This chapter is followed by selections from the archetypal Chinese novels:

Romance of the Three Kingdoms, Water Margin, Journey to the West, Chin P'ing Mei, The Scholars, and *Dream of the Red Chamber.* The representative selections from modern fiction include stories by Lu Hsün (nos. **133, 134**), Yü Ta-fu, Mao Tun (nos. **135, 136**), Lao She (nos. **137, 138**), Shen Ts'ung-wen and Chao Shu-li (no. **141**).

Both chapters and individual entries are provided with informative and explanatory introductions. The carefully selected translations are faithful to the original, preserving many of the qualities distinctly Chinese. This anthology is highly recommended to the reader who is without a previous background in Chinese literature.

25. Li, Dun J., ed. and tr. *The Essence of Chinese Civilization.* Paperbound. Princeton: Van Nostrand Reinhold Co., 1967. xx, 476 pp.

This anthology is a comprehensive collection of 200 excerpts from a number of major and minor works by Chinese authors. Well organized, with excellent selections for its purpose, the translations depict traditional Chinese civilization. The book is divided topically into four major parts: philosophy and religion, government, economics, and family and society. The usually accurate translations are refreshingly clear—close to the originals and yet easily read and understood. The addition of relevant explanatory notes on the same page as the translation increases the usefulness of the anthology for the general reader, and the inclusion of bibliographical data is of value to the scholar. (Unfortunately an index with the Chinese characters is not provided.) Additional aids are descriptive tables of contents, map, chronological table, pronunciation guide, and index. Although the book is not exclusively designed for an audience with literary interests, a large number of the selections have not been previously translated and many are by major prose stylists.

Classics

26. Legge, James, ed. and tr. *The Chinese Classics.* Reprinted with minor corrections and added concordance. 5 vols. and supplement. Hong Kong: Hong Kong University Press, 1960. 508, 610, 750, 812 and 954 pp.

James Legge's translation of the Chinese Classics is the English classic of Sinology and has helped train several generations of Western scholars. First published between 1861 and 1872, the work, intended to include the *Four Books* and Five Classics, is actually incomplete—the *Book of Changes* (the R. Wilhelm translation is preferred, see no. **27**) and the *Book of Ritual* (of lesser interest from the literary standpoint) were later published in 1882 and 1885 in Max Müller's *Sacred Books of the East,* the former recently reprinted in two different editions. Legge supplements his masterful translations with an enormous amount of auxiliary material, including very complete introductions, thorough annotations, indices, partial concordances, and the complete Chinese texts in a most convenient format.

The *Analects, Great Learning,* and *Doctrine of the Mean* found in volume one and the *Mencius* in volume two comprise the *Four Books.* Volume three contains the *Book of Documents;* four, the *Book of Odes;* and five, *The Spring and Autumn Annals* with the *Tso chuan* commentary. Each of the preceding will be discussed in separate entries. Although Legge uses a sometimes stiff Victorian prose style and a system of romanization no longer accepted, it remains the standard work by which subsequent translations of the Classics have been judged.

27. *I Ching. The I Ching (or Book of Changes).* Tr. and extensively annot. by Richard Wilhelm. Tr. from German to English by Cary F. Baynes (1950). 3d ed. Bollingen Series, vol. 19. Princeton: Princeton University Press, 1967. 740 pp.

28. Wilhelm, Hellmut. *Change, Eight Lectures on the "I Ching".* Tr. by Cary F. Baynes. Bollingen Series, vol. 62. New York: Pantheon Books, 1960. x,111 pp. (Paperback, Harper Torchbooks).

One of the Five Classics of the Confucian canon, the *I ching* consists of a manual of divination—the basic text, and ten "Wings"—several sorts of commentaries to the text. The text itself is one of the earliest extant Chinese works, if not the earliest; according to tradition, it was written by King Wen, the founder of the Chou dynasty. Although the Wings have traditionally been attributed to Confucius and his disciples, they are of later date, written variously in the late Chou and early Han periods.

The manual portion consists of short oracles arranged under sixty-four hexagrams, symbols composed of broken and unbroken lines in combinations of six. Divining stalks were cast in a series, even numbers representing broken lines and odd numbers unbroken, until a particular hexagram was developed. Referring to the manual, the diviner could then consult the relevant oracle, which was written in a terse and ambiguous fashion. For example, the oracle to the first hexagram begins, "The creature works sublime success/ Furthering through perseverance."

The Wings move beyond simple divination and invest the work with philosophical import, providing examples of early Chinese cosmological and metaphysical speculation. The entire universe is characterized by continual change and the wise man must understand these changes in order to achieve success. Divination through the hexagrams enables him to understand the present situation and thus determine his course of action.

First published in 1924, Richard Wilhelm's translation, a product of his excellent scholarship and intense involvement with the work, is still the best translation available. An extensive commentary follows every few lines of translation, enabling the reader to comprehend one interpretation of the work. Additional aids in the third edition include seventeen pages of preface and introduction by Richard Wilhelm with detailed instructions on how to use the work for the purpose of divination; five pages of translation notes by C. F. Baynes; a foreword by C. G. Jung on the psychological implications of the *I ching*; and an eight-page foreword to the third edition by Hellmut Wilhelm, the translator's son and an important Chinese scholar in his own right.

It should be understood that due to the ambiguity of the *I ching*, any reading in the original Chinese or a translation is to be considered an interpretation. Although Wilhelm's translation is still the recommended one, much research has been done since the early 1920s. Considering the antiquity of the earliest portion of the *I ching*, studies of the Shang oracle bone inscriptions have added new possibilities to understanding the work. It is quite possible that in the future, new translations will be published that radically alter the traditional interpretations of these early passages.

In Peking in 1943 during the Japanese occupation, Hellmut Wilhelm gave a series of eight lectures, later published under the title, *Change, Eight Lectures on the "I Ching"*. This slim volume concerns itself with the contents of the *I ching*, its date and authorship (maintaining a rather conservative position), the basic concept of the work, its metaphysical and cosmological aspects, a detailed explanation of the text and commentaries, a general survey of studies on the *I ching* throughout Chinese history, and the uses of the work in Chinese life. The result of excellent scholarship, this work is of immense value in guiding the reader towards an understanding of the *I ching*.

29. *Shu ching. The Book of Documents.* Ed. and tr. by Bernard Karlgren. Reprint from Bulletin 22. Stockholm: Museum of Far Eastern Antiquities, 1950. 81 pp.

The *Shu ching* (Book of Documents), the oldest Chinese "history," is a collection of separate documents without any connecting narrative or reference from one document to the other. The earliest of these documents is theoretically from the reign of the legendary Emperor Yao; the latest concerns events of 626 B.C. The work may actually be divided into two parts: the "Old Text" (so named because it was first found in an archaic form of script), which is mainly a Han dynasty compilation, and the " New Text," which is considered genuine. The latter, together with the *I ching* (Book of Changes) and *Shih ching* (Book of Odes), form the oldest strata of Chinese literature, dating from the end of the Shang dynasty to the middle of the Chou.

Most of the documents consist of direct speech, a technique

which became common in subsequent Chinese histories. Those supposedly written by the Duke of Chou, the most important documents in the *Shu*, are quite likely genuine. The Duke of Chou was the younger brother and prime minister to King Wu, the founder of the Chou dynasty and, following King Wu's death, regent to Wu's young son, Ch'eng. These speeches record the method by which the Duke of Chou was able to secure the rule of the Chou dynasty following the conquest of the Shang. The philosophy espoused in these particular documents later became a major aspect of Confucian thought.

Because the *Shu* is such an early composition, it is exceedingly difficult to read: passages are missing or unintelligible, and the style and vocabulary are often quite different from later Chinese literature. The translation of the older "New Text" section by Bernhard Karlgren, a pioneering scholar of early Chinese, is the product of many years of painstaking research. Highly literal, the translation was published primarily for the use of scholars and contains the Chinese text; but, because the fascination of the *Shu* as literature lies in its terseness and archaic quality, Karlgen's literal translation is most effective.

30. *Ch'un ch'iu. The "Ch'un ch'iu" with the "Tso chuan"*. Tr. by James Legge. In *The Chinese Classics*, vol. 5. (See no. 26).

The various states during the Chou dynasty maintained chronicles of events, but only three have survived. The most famous one, which has become one of the Five Classics, is that of the state of Lu, covering the period 722–481 B.C. Because Confucius was a native of the state of Lu, this work as well as the rest of the Classics has been traditionally ascribed to him. Compiled on a month-to-month basis, the work is called *Ch'un ch'iu*, or *Spring and Autumn Annals*. These chronological records are brief, often to the point of obscurity.

Three commentaries interpreting the records from the standpoint of Confucian morality were appended to the *Ch'un ch'iu*. The most important is the *Tso chuan* or the *Tso Commentary*. Although the original form and authorship of the *Tso chuan* remain controversial problems, it seems to have been a separate history which was later chopped up and revised to fit the *Ch'un ch'iu*. The *Ch'un ch'iu* alone does not provide adequate information for an understanding of the historical period it covers. It is the *Tso chuan*, even though it undoubtedly includes fictional material, that portrays the age.

Aside from its importance as history, the *Tso chuan* is most important in the development of Chinese literature as it is the first work to present sustained narrative and imagery. Written in a terse style, it seeks to convey not only a record of events but their mood as well. Here is a description of a desperate retreat across a river: "The army of the center and of the 3rd army struggled for the boats, till the fingers [of those trying to get in that were cut off by those who had already got possession] could be taken up with both hands at once." As one of the originators of the primarily didactic nature of Chinese history, the *Tso chuan* renders judgment on historical figures, and is concerned with the moral consequences of historical events. For example, where the *Ch'un ch'iu* records, "In autumn, Duke Chuang of Chu was buried" (507 B.C.), the *Tso chuan* provides a description of Chuang's death and an analysis of his character:

The Duke of Chu was on the terrace at the top of the palace gate, looking down into his courtyard. The gateekeeper at the time was dousing the courtyard with water from a pitcher. The duke, spying him from afar, was greatly annoyed. When he questioned the gatekeeper, the latter explained, "Lord I Yeh-ku pissed in the court there!"

The duke ordered I Yeh-ku arrested. When I Yeh-ku could not be found, the duke, more furious than ever, flung himself down on his bed with such violence that he fell off into the ashes of the brazier and burned to death.... Duke Chuang was a very impetuous and fastidious man, and therefore he came to such an end. (Duke Ting, 3, [507 B.C.].) [Tr. by Burton Watson, *Early Chinese Literature*, pp. 65–66; cf. Legge, p. 747]

The translation by James Legge, the only complete one in English, unfortunately relegated the *Tso chuan* to a mere commentary to the *Ch'un ch'iu*, and printed it in small type along with the other notes and comments. Hence, the Legge version is difficult to read and appreciate. It is hoped that a modern translation will eventually be produced.

31. *Ta hsüeh* and *Chung yung. The Great Learning and the Mean-in Action.* Tr. with intro. by E. R. Hughes. New York: E. P. Dutton & Co., 1943, xi, 176 pp.

The *Ta hsüeh* (Great Learning) and *Chung yung* (Doctrine of the Mean) are two short but important philosophical chapters from the *Li chi* (Book of Rites), one of the Five Classics. In the Sung dynasty, the *Ta hsüeh* and *Chung yung* were combined with the *Analects* and the *Mencius* to form the collection known as the *Four Books*, the basic texts of Neo-Confucian philosophy and the civil service examinations. The *Ta hsüeh* concerns itself with moral cultivation and social order; the *Chung yung*, with the most religious and mystical philosophy to be found among the basic Confucian texts.

Translations of the *Ta hsüeh* and *Chung yung* are only a small part of the volume by E. R. Hughes. His 104-page introduction includes an interesting essay on the philosophical influence of these texts upon European intellectual history, along with a study of their authorship. The translations contain extensive additional commentary and interpretation, the entire work designed to thoroughly elucidate the material for the general reader.

History

32. Beasley, W. G., and Pulleyblank, E. G., eds. *Historians of China and Japan*. New York and London: Oxford University Press, 1961. vi, 351 pp.

Ten of the eighteen articles in this volume by authorities on Chinese and Japanese historiography concern themselves with China. Of especial interest, as they deal with historians and historical works separately cited in this guide, are A. F. P. Hulsewé's "Notes on the Historiography of the Han Period," which includes discussion of Ssu-ma Ch'ien and Pan Ku; and E. G. Pulleyblank's "Chinese Historical Criticism: Liu Chih-chi and Ssu-ma Kuang," which considers the methods used by Ssu-ma Kuang in writing his *Tzu-chih t'ung-chien* (no. **39**). Recommended also are Yang Lien-sheng's "The Organization of Chinese Official Historiography: Principles and Methods of the Standard Histories from the T'ang through the Ming Dynasty," and J. Gray's "Historical Writing in Twentieth-century China: Notes on its Background and Development," which provides an excellent summary of the development of modern Chinese historiography.

33. Crump, J. I. *Intrigues: Studies of the "Chan-kuo Ts'e"*. Ann Arbor: University of Michigan Press, 1964. x, 212 pp.

34. *Chan-kuo Ts'e*. Tr. by J. I. Crump, Jr. Oxford: Clarendon Press, 1970. xxviii, 602 pp.

Although the *Chan-kuo ts'e* (Intrigues of the Warring States), lending its name to the Warring States period (403–221 B.C.), is not in itself a work of history, it is one of the most important sources for the history of the fifth through third centuries B.C. in China, and has been treated as a historical work since the Han dynasty. The work is primarily a handbook on rhetoric and persuasive speaking utilizing examples from history. Divided into sections corresponding to the twelve states of the time, the anecdotes in each are arranged in approximate chronological order. As with the few other historical works of the Chou dynasty, the author(s) is unknown; it probably dates from the early part of the second century B.C., although Crump believes the work to have been edited into its present form by Liu Hsiang (80–9 B.C., first major bibliographer) no later than 8 B.C.

The material of the *Chan-kuo ts'e* is presented in at least three varied forms: state documents, anecdotes and stories, and diplomatic dialogues. Many of the anecdotes follow a set pattern, beginning with a problem, followed by a speaker who persuades the ruler into an appropriate course of action, and ending with a brief mention concerning the success of the speaker's persuasiveness and his proposal. As is to be expected, the advice of the speaker is usually followed and turns out to have been the best solution. Since the emphasis is on the persuasiveness of rhetoric, the work is marked by a tone of cynicism and unscrupulousness. It is for this reason that the work has been rather neglected in the history of Chinese literature.

Intrigues is a partial translation of fifty pieces, about ten percent of the original text, selected as "examples of superior Chinese prose . . . compared and examined for internal evidence of their writers' habit of mind." The translations are arranged according to the central theme of the anecdotes into nine chapters. These themes include aspects of the social and political life of the Chan-kuo period, literary styles, and the traditions of persuasiveness and of rhetoric. The author stresses the fictional and rhetorical aspects of the *Chan-kuo ts'e*, attempting to "remove a work from the realm of history and give it to fiction." For the scholar there is extensive material to supplement the translations and commentary—various finding lists, translation notes, a bibliography, and an index with characters.

A complete, eminently readable translation of the *Chan-kuo ts'e* has recently been published as part of the "Oxford Library of East Asian Literatures," edited by David Hawkes. Crump has successfully struck a fine balance between the needs of the general reader and the needs of the scholar. The lucid translation avoids unnecessary footnotes and admits implied words essential for English intelligibility without brackets, while each passage is identified by references to the most important Chinese editions. The footnotes, written in a terse but free and personal style, are at the bottom of each page with the essential Chinese characters. A bibliography, and an alphabetical finding list based on the romanized opening words of the Chinese text for each passage, complete this long-awaited work.

35. Ssu-ma Ch'ien. *Records of the Grand Historian of China (Shih chi)*. Tr. by Burton Watson. 2 vols. New York: Columbia University Press, 1961. xi, 563 pp. and viii, 543 pp. (Abridged paperback edition).

36. Watson, Burton. *Ssu-ma Ch'ien: Grand Historian of China*. New York: Columbia University Press, 1958. xi, 276 pp.

The *Shih chi*, by Ssu-ma Ch'ien (ca. 145–ca. 90 B.C), is the first Chinese history for which the date of compilation and authorship are known. It is China's most important history, and one of the great early histories in the literature of the world. History-writing is often considered one of China's major contributions to the world: much of the credit toward this development must go to Ssu-ma Ch'ien.

Ssu-ma T'an (d. 110 B.C.), Ssu-ma Ch'ien's father, was an astrologer-astronomer at the court of Emperor Wu of the Han dynasty (reigned 140–88 B.C.). He had begun a history of unknown scope and at his death charged his son to complete this work. Ssu-ma Ch'ien succeeded to his father's post and continued work on the history. Before finishing the history, because he sided with a general who had surrendered to the enemy when expected reinforcements failed to appear due to lack of support by the emperor, Ssu-ma Ch'ien was condemned to be castrated. Rather than commit suicide as was expected in such circumstances, he endured the punishment and the subsequent shame in order to complete his history.

Ssu-ma Ch'ien envisioned his work as a history of the entire world as known to the Chinese of his time, from the beginning of civilization to his own day. He arranged the 130 chapters of his history into five divisions: twelve "Basic Annals," dealing with ruling dynasties and individual rulers; ten "Chronological Tables," listing in graph form the principal events in the various fiefs and feudal states; eight "Treatises," covering such subjects as rites, music, astronomy, economics, and religious affairs; thirty chapters on the "Hereditary Houses" of the Chou and

Han periods; and seventy chapters of "Biographies," ending with an autobiography of the author. The last division includes biographies not only of famous statesmen, generals, and philosophers, with accounts of foreign lands and peoples, but also of the lives of fortune-tellers, famous assassins, humorists, and big businessmen, thus providing along with the political history an overall view of the various historical periods. The emphasis on biography continues the tendency of the earlier histories to view the individual in interaction with society as the determining factor in the course of history.

The Chinese historian, viewing himself as a transmitter and a conservator of past tradition, compiles his history by incorporating previous histories almost verbatim whenever possible in his narrative. Ssu-ma Ch'ien continued this practice by compiling and weaving together accounts taken from earlier works, setting off his comments and interpretations at the end of each section with the phrase, "The Grand Historian remarks." These remarks contain additional material, discuss the narrative's reliability, attempt to ascertain the course of events, or present the historian's personal views and moral judgments, and are often the most interesting parts of the history. Ssu-ma Ch'ien's originality is not only apparent in his innovations in the form of history-writing and in his comments, but also in his prose, which is unusual in being highly personal. Since his time, the *Shih chi* has been read by every educated Chinese as the definitive record of early Chinese history, as well as for the pleasure of reading Ssu-ma Ch'ien's narrative.

Burton Watson's translation covers the most reliable part of the *Shih chi*, those sections dealing with the Han dynasty. Volume I covers the early years from 209 to 141 B.C. Since Ssu-ma Ch'ien divided his material of any one period into several sections, the whole of the history has to be read to form a complete picture of any particular chronological period. In the first volume, Watson has extracted chapters from various sections and rearranged them to cover the early Han dynasty. Volume II deals with the age of Emperor Wu from 140 to about 100 B.C., providing translations of several treatises and a number of biographies, including complete translations of seven type-biography chapters; e.g. "Harsh Officials," "Wandering Knights," "Money-makers." The general reader with limited time may find the second volume of greater literary interest.

For a fuller introduction to Ssu-ma Ch'ien and the *Shih chi*, Burton Watson's *Ssu-ma Ch'ien: Grand Historian of China* is recommended. Watson's lucid and persuasive account of the times, life and thought of Ssu-ma Ch'ien and early Chinese historiography should interest layman and specialist alike.

37. Ssu-ma Ch'ien. *Statesman, Patriot, and General in Ancient China: Three "Shih chi" Biographies of the Ch'in Dynasty (255–206 B.C.).* Tr. and discussed by Derk Bodde. New Haven: American Oriental Society, 1940. xi, 75 pp. (Paperback, Kraus Reprint Co.).

This volume of translations supplements Derk Bodde's earlier work, *China's First Unifier, A Study of the Ch'in dynasty as seen in the Life of Li Ssu (280–208 B.C.),* (Sinica Leidensia Series, vol. 3; Leiden, 1938), in presenting an overall view of the Ch'in dynasty. For the general reader the work is of value as it presents in a slim volume historically related biographies from the *Shih chi* of three different and interesting figures. Each highly readable translation is followed by a textual and historical study of the *Shih chi* account.

The first biography is of a wealthy merchant, Lü Pu-wei (d. 235 B.C.), who sponsored a minor prince of the state of Ch'in and intrigued to make him crown prince. At the crown prince's request, Lü gave him his courtesan-concubine who, already pregnant, presented the crown prince with an heir. (As Bodde points out in his following discussion, this aspect of the story is probably a later fabrication.) This child eventually became Ch'in Shih Huang Ti, the first emperor of China. When the crown prince became king, he made Lü Pu-wei his Grand Counsellor and bestowed on him a number of high honors. The king had been on the throne but three years when he died, leaving the throne to his (Lü Pu-wei's) son. Lü Pu-wei rose to the highest state office, had secret relations with the Queen-Dowager, and then provided her with an escort of unusual physical dimensions. Eventually he fell from the king's favor and committed suicide.

The biography of Ching K'o (d. 227 B.C.) is found in the *Shih chi* together with the biographies of four other noted political assassins of earlier periods. The state of Ch'in was rapidly expanding at this time and threatened the state of Yen. Ching K'o, who had a reputation as a swordsman, was induced to assassinate the king of Ch'in. To stimulate the courage of Ching K'o and carry out the plan, other brave men sacrificed their lives. Ching K'o was able to approach within striking distance of the king of Ch'in, but at the last minute he bungled the job. The description of the assassination scene is a descriptive *tour de force*, combining both pathos and slapstick humor.

Meng T'ien (d. 210 B.C.), the subject of the last biography, was the most famous Ch'in general, known chiefly as the builder of the Great Wall. In the intrigues that followed the death of the First Emperor of Ch'in he was forced to commit suicide.

38. Pan Ku. *The History of the Former Han Dynasty*. Tr. and annot. by Homer H. Dubs. 3 vols. New York: American Council of Learned Societies, 1938–1955. xii, 339; ix, 426; and xiv, 563 pp. (Distr. by Spoken Language Services, Ithaca, N.Y.).

After the death of the usurper Wang Mang and the re-establishment of the Han dynasty in A.D. 25, Pan Piao (A.D. 3–54) began a work on the history of the latter part of the Former Han dynasty as a continuation of the *Shih chi* (no. 35–37). Following his death, his son Pan Ku (A.D. 32–92) continued the work, expanding it to cover the whole of the Former Han period as well as the reign of the usurper Wang Mang; i.e., the period from 209 B.C to A.D. 25. Like Ssu-ma Ch'ien, he encountered political difficulties before he completed the history. He was jailed because of his association with a general accused of treason, and died in prison. His sister, Pan Chao (died ca. 116), was commissioned by the emperor to complete his work, but the bulk of the history as well as its form and method was the work of Pan Ku.

Pan Ku adopted the form created by Ssu-ma Ch'ien with only slight modification, dividing his material of 100 chapters into "Imperial Annals," "Treatises," "Chronological Tables" and "Biographies"; the "Hereditary House" section, no longer relevant, was dropped. New topics were added to the "Treatises" section, such as geography and bibliography. The history, entitled the *Han shu* (History of the Former Han), became the model for succeeding histories, most of which were limited to the span of a single dynasty. A tradition developed whereby each succeeding dynasty commissioned a history of the preceding one. This led to the view of Chinese history as a succession of dynasties with the result that the time between dynasties, often the most creative periods, tended to be ignored.

Following the tradition of Chinese historiography, almost half of the material in the *Han shu* was copied nearly verbatim from the *Shih chi*, demonstrating Pan Ku's trust of Ssu-ma Ch'ien's work. Occasionally, new material was added and Pan Ku altered Ssu-ma Ch'ien's style to fit his own less personal, more conventional prose. For this reason, his rendition is often more easily read than the original. Pan Ku also was less subjective than Ssu-ma Ch'ien, his remarks conforming to the dominant Confucian doctrine of his age.

The three-volume translation by Homer Dubs includes all of the "Imperial Annals" section, beginning with the birth of Liu Pang, the founder of the Han dynasty, in 248 B.C., and ending with the death of Wang Mang in A.D. 25 and important passages from "The Treatise on Food and Goods" that concern Wang Mang. The translation of each chapter from the *Han shu* begins with an extensive introduction and summary of the period and often ends with one or more appendices dealing with subjects of interest. The excellent and thoroughly researched translation includes the Chinese text and extensive notes. Although Dubs's work is of greatest value to the scholar, his well-organized and highly readable translation will provide the general reader with a major section of the second most important example of Chinese historical prose.

39. Ssu-ma Kuang. *The Chronicle of the Three Kingdoms (220–265): Chapters 69–78 from the "Tzu Chih T'ung Chien."*

Tr. and annot. by Achilles Fang. 2 vols. (1952). Vol. 1, ed. by Glen W. Baxter; vol. 2, ed. by Bernard S. Soloman. Harvard-Yenching Institute Studies, vol. 6. Paperbound. Cambridge: Harvard University Press, 1965. xx, 714 and ix, 693 pp.

Ssu-ma Kuang (1019–1086), one of the most important scholar-officials of the Sung dynasty, completed the *Tzu-chih t'ung-chien* (Comprehensive Mirror for Aid in Government) in 1084 after nineteen years of effort. Although most Chinese histories after the *Han shu* (no. **38**) were written to cover one dynasty and were government-sponsored, private scholars occasionally wrote more comprehensive histories. Ssu-ma Kuang's chronicle is the most ambitious of all individual works up to his own time, being a complete history of China from 403 B.C. to A.D. 959, covering a period of 1,362 years. Because of its excellence in both style and organization, it became one of the basic readings for the Chinese intellectual.

The 294 chapters of the history are arranged completely according to chronological sequence rather than by sections with the internal sequential arrangements of previous Chinese histories. Although privately written, Ssu-ma Kuang's history received government encouragement and financial support. The method of compilation is of interest because of its well-thought-out system. A skeleton outline was first written, followed by a "Long Draft." This was then abridged with commentary to form the history itself. Subsequently, "Examination of Differences" was written, consisting of notes on discrepancies between the sources (over 300) for various passages in the history.

The translation by Achilles Fang of chapters 69–78 covering the Three Kingdoms period (A.D. 220–265) is the major Western-language work on this time span. Fang's translation is a monumental work of scholarship in that every source for the history is noted and commented upon. The 153-page index (at the end of vol. 2) itself is a major contribution to further research. The general reader is likely to encounter some difficulty in following the translation, as it closely follows the Chinese original and (fortunately for the specialist) includes the Chinese equivalents of all proper names, difficult passages, and important quotations. However, the clarity of the translation will enable him to become familiar with a portion of one of the most important Chinese histories by a famous prose stylist.

40. Fa-hsien. *The Travels of Fa-hsien (399–414 A.D.)*, or *Record of the Buddhistic Kingdoms*. (1923). Tr. (2d version) by H. A. Giles. London: Routledge and Kegan Paul, 1959. xiv, 96 pp.

41. Hsüan-tsang. *Si-Yu-Ki: Buddhist Records of the Western World*. Tr. by Samuel Beal. 2 vols. Trübners' Oriental Series. London: K. Paul, Trench, Trübner, 1906. cviii, 242 and 369 pp. (Reprinted by S. Gupta, Calcutta, in 4 vols., 1957 and 1958).

42. Waley, Arthur, tr. *The Real Tripitaka and Other Pieces*. London: George Allen & Unwin; New York: Macmillan Co., 1952. 291 pp.

As Buddhism grew in importance in China, a number of Chinese monks seeking knowledge of doctrine and Sanskrit from the mother-country of Buddhism journeyed to India to visit holy sites, and to bring back sacred texts and relics. Some of these pilgrims wrote accounts of their travels. Beyond their intrinsic interest, these detailed records are important as major sources of Indian history.

Fa-hsien is the first important Chinese pilgrim, being the first to succeed in reaching India, remain there for an extensive period, and return to China. In 399, he journeyed to India by way of the deserts and mountains of Central Asia, visited a number of places in India, and having accomplished his purpose of obtaining certain texts, planned to return to China by sea. On his return voyage, he stopped in Ceylon, where he spent two years. Encountering difficulties after leaving Ceylon, he spent over two hundred days at sea before reaching southern China in 414. On his return, he recorded his journey. Giles's literal translation of this record is quite readable but unfortunately, so as not to "check the enjoyment of the reader as he travels along with Fa-hsien on his stupendous journey," explanatory footnotes were omitted. The volume lacks as well a satisfactory introduction, although it does include a map of the journey.

Hsüan-tsang (ca. 596–664) is the most famous pilgrim as well as one of the most important figures in the history of Chinese Buddhism. The record of his travels, the *Hsi yu chi* (Record of the Western Region), became the basis for a major Chinese novel (see nos. **103–105**). Although his petition to the court for permission to leave China had been refused, Hsüan-tsang secretly left for India in 629. After an arduous journey and a series of adventures—becoming lost in the desert, encountering a king who wished to detain him against his will and bandits who wanted to offer him as a human sacrifice—Hsüan-tsang reached Kashmir where he studied for two years, travelled through India visiting the important Buddhist holy places, and then sojourned at the great Buddhist university at Nalanda. By the time he had finished a second stay at the university, his reputation had spread throughout India and Hsüan-tsang was honored by the Indian emperors and rulers of the day. After an absence of sixteen years, Hsüan-tsang returned in 645 to Ch'ang-an, the capital of T'ang dynasty China, where he was given a hero's welcome and became a favorite of the Emperor. He had brought back hundreds of sutras and began their translation into Chinese. Many of his translations are still the standard ones.

Samuel Beal's translation is partially based on Stanislas Julien's translation into French published in the middle of the nineteenth century; at that time the Western study of Chinese Buddhism was in its infancy. Aside from the problem of the accuracy of the translation, the general reader is likely to find the detailed description of the sites visited by Hsüan-tsang of little interest, although they have been of immense aid in studying the geography and history of India. Beal also includes translations of the travels of Fa-hsien and two other pilgrims in his introduction.

Arthur Waley's excellent abridged work on the life and travels of Hsüan-tsang, "The Real Tripitaka," should be of greater interest. This volume is divided into five parts. The first part is the above-mentioned piece and the second part continues the history of Buddhism in China with the story of two Japanese monks, Ennin and Ensai, who travelled to China as the Chinese journeyed to India. One long eighteenth-century story and seven short ninth-century stories are translated in Waley's usual superb fashion in part three. Part four contains two miscellaneous Japanese pieces and part five contains three original stories in Chinese style by Arthur Waley, including a new chapter to the novel, *Hsi yu chi* (see no. **103** for Arthur Waley's translation of this novel).

43. Giles, Lionel, tr. *A Gallery of Chinese Immortals: Selected Biographies.* Wisdom of the East Series. London: John Murray, 1948. 128 pp.

Lionel Giles has selected from a variety of sources fictional biographies of *hsien* from the legendary periods through the T'ang dynasty. The Chinese character *hsien* is composed of the pictographic elements for man and for mountain; hence, it originally meant a hermit. Eventually the term came to refer to a person who has greatly increased his life span, an immortal without the Western connotation of infinite life. Toward the end of the Chou dynasty, there developed a form of Taoism that was interested in prolonging life through diet, breathing procedures, special exercises, sexual practices, and especially, types of medication. From this interest, there developed a delightful literature concerning the legendary successful practitioners.

The following is a brief example of the great variety of stories included in the collection:

Tu Tzu ("Master Calf") was a native of Yeh. As a young man, he used to gather fir-cones and fu-ling (tubers of *Pachyma cocos,* a fungus growth upon the roots of fir-trees) on the Black Mountain to diet himself with. For several hundred years he alternated between robust youth and old age, good looks and ugliness, so that he came to be recognized as a hsien. His usual round took him past the establishment of the vintner Yang Tu, whose daughter sold wine in the marketplace. Her eyebrows met in the middle, and her ears were long and delicate. These marks were considered extraordinary, and everybody declared that she was a celestial being.

Now Tu Tzu, while he was leading a yellow calf along the road, happened to meet Yang Tu's daughter, and was so delighted with the girl that he arranged to keep her as his handmaid. She, therefore, went out in Tu Tzu's company to gather peaches and plums. They would spend one night away and then return with a number of sacks full of fruit. People in the town tried to follow and keep a watch on them, but although they went out of the gate together, still leading the calf, no runner was able to overtake them, and there was nothing for it but to return.

The couple continued to frequent the market-place for thirty years or more, and then they departed. They have been seen at the foot of Mt. P'an selling their peaches and plums in winter. [pp. 22–23]

Philosophy

44. Creel, H. G. *Chinese Thought from Confucius to Mao Tse-tung.* Chicago: University of Chicago Press, 1953; London: Eyre and Spottiswoods, 1954. 292 pp. (Paperback, Mentor Books).

This most readable volume is the best introduction to a general survey of Chinese thought available. Especially useful is Creel's presentation of the material. Various philosophies are considered within the context of the historical situations in which they arose. Unfortunately, while the handling of the material up to the turn of the era is excellent, the last two thousand years of Chinese thought are not adequately covered: thirty pages are provided for both Buddhism and Neo-Confucianism, the predominant philosophies from the fourth through the seventeenth centuries; Neo-Taoism, important in the third through fifth centuries, is completely ignored. The work ends with suggestions for further readings, a bibliography, and textual references.

45. Chan Wing-tsit. *A Source Book in Chinese Philosophy.* Princeton: Princeton University Press, 1963. xxv, 856 pp. (Paperback).

This compendium of translations is a milestone in Western studies on Chinese philosophy. Chan Wing-tsit, one of the important scholars of Chinese philosophy in the United States, has been well aware of the great need for the work he has produced—translations of the basic Chinese philosophical works from the earliest texts to the present, including important works that have not previously been translated. The volume took Chan many years to complete, as all of the translations are his own. This was not done for internal consistency alone; many past translations were either out-of-date or did not utilize the important Chinese commentaries to the works. Hence, the book is of value to both beginning and advanced students. The introductions which precede each of the selections can, as a whole, serve as an introductory history of Chinese philosophy. The works translated were chosen for their importance within the development of Chinese thought and to strike a balance between the various schools and periods of Chinese philosophy. Of course, in a work of this extent, some disagreement with aspects of the translations is unavoidable. One criticism is that many of the translations of early texts follow Neo-Confucian interpretations. This is not surprising in view of the fact that Chan is one of the two foremost scholars of Neo-Confucian philosophy in the West. Another criticism is that a number of selections from important works appear to have been chosen for their similarity to Western philosophical concepts rather than for their importance within the development of Chinese thought.

Well-written, with lucid translations, and embodying excellent scholarship, this volume is highly recommended. The *Source Book* includes an interesting appendix on translating certain Chinese philosophical terms, a helpful bibliography, and an extensive glossary of Chinese characters, as well as an index.

46. Waley, Arthur, tr. *Three Ways of Thought in Ancient China.* (1939). New York: Barnes and Noble, 1953. 275 pp. (Paperback, Anchor Books).

This book consists primarily of selections from three works: *Chuang-tzu, Mencius,* and *Han Fei-tzu* (see individual entries in this section), representative texts of the most important schools of Chinese thought competing in the Late Chou period (fifth through third centuries B.C.). Arthur Waley selected the passages and translated them for the general reader, so the work is not only informative, but also enjoyable to read. The selections from the *Chuang-tzu* will appeal to the reader's imagination; the *Mencius,* to one's moral feelings; and readers are likely to find in the fewer selections from the *Han Fei-tzu* a political philosophy one might be tempted to compare with the philosophy of the present century. This book is recommended as the first volume of translations to be read by the layman and for use in general introductory courses.

47. *The Analects of Confucius.* Tr. and annot. by Arthur Waley.

London: George Allen & Unwin, 1938; New York: Random House, 1938. 268 pp. (Paperback, Modern Library).

48. Creel, H. G. *Confucius: The Man and the Myth.* New York: John Day Co., 1949; London: Routledge and Kegan Paul, 1951. 363 pp. (Paperback retitled *Confucius and the Chinese Way,* Harper).

The *Analects* is one of the most difficult of Chinese works for the Western reader to appreciate; yet, since it is considered the most important philosophical text in China, it cannot be lightly dismissed. The book of twenty chapters consists of reminiscences of the teachings of Confucius (d. 478 B.C.) by his disciples and their students. Taking the form of random statements, answers to questions, and brief dialogues, the reminiscences are written in the very terse style characteristic of early Chinese. Because these passages often have no context, they are difficult to interpret and are sometimes quite ambiguous. Added to this difficulty is the problem of dealing with a number of passages that have crept into the *Analects* that were written by others after Confucius and even encompass philosophies opposite to his own.

Even when the difficulties in approaching the text are overcome and an understanding of the historical context is gained, Western readers often still fail to acquire the Chinese and Japanese appreciation of the *Analects.* James Legge, in the prolegomena to his translation of the *Analects,* published in 1861, wrote: "I must now leave the sage. I hope I have not done him injustice; but after long study of his character and opinions, I am unable to regard him as a great man." In preparing the second edition, some thirty years later, Legge found almost nothing to change in his translation, but he revised the above to read: "The more I have studied his character and opinions, the more highly have I come to regard him. He was a very great man." Like fine Bordeaux, the *Analects* seems to improve with age and maturity; one should not feel discouraged should a first reading prove disappointing.

The highly readable and thoroughly researched translation by Arthur Waley is the recommended one. However, because of the great difficulties in interpreting the *Analects* (all translations are by nature interpretations), it is also recommended that Waley's translation be used together with James Legge's *(The Chinese Classics,* no. **26)** for purposes of comparison. The translation by Waley includes an extensive introduction that should be especially useful to the general reader, with a discussion of the important terms used in the *Analects.* For a more thorough introduction to the life, times and thought of Confucius, H. G. Creel's somewhat controversial work is most valuable.

49. Mencius. *Mencius.* Tr. by D. C. Lau. Paperbound. Baltimore: Penguin Books, 1970. 280 pp.

50. ———. *The Mencius.* Tr. by James Legge. Available in a number of different editions. (See also entry no. **26**).

51. ———. *The Mencius.* Tr. by W.A.C.H. Dobson. Toronto: University of Toronto Press, 1963. xviii, 215 pp. (Paperback).

Mencius (372–289 B.C.) was one of the two most significant followers of Confucius. (The other was Hsün-tzu, see nos. **55–57.**) Following the selection by Chu Hsi (A.D. 1130–1200) of the *Mencius* as one of the *Four Books* (together with the *Analects* and two chapters from the *Book of Rites*—see separate entries) and its incorporation into the official Thirteen Classics, it became one of the most important of all Chinese books.

With the *Mencius,* a major step was taken in the development of Chinese prose. This work of seven chapters is composed of dialogues of varying length, usually exchanges between Mencius and a feudal ruler, written for the purpose of presenting an argument and point of view. Although it is difficult to ascertain the historical basis of these interviews, they are written in a refreshing anecdotal manner that gives the impression of actual conversation. The *Mencius* never lapses into the tedious tone and style of some of the other works of the time and is therefore a pleasure to read.

Aside from its literary value, the *Mencius* is of major philosophical import. Following the Sung dynasty, the *Mencius* became the accepted interpretation of the teachings of Confucius. The *Mencius* provides a fuller understanding of early Confucianism than does the *Analects*; it is easier to read and its arguments are complete and clearly stated. Certain of Mencius' views—for example, the view that economic planning is essential to a stable society—are remarkably in accord with contemporary Western thought. Mencius is also renowned for his view of human nature; in contrast to Hsün-tzu, he believed that man is innately good.

The translation by James Legge is literal. Dobson, in his stilted translation, takes liberties and often paraphrases. He has systematically rearranged the contents by topic, and his work is preceded by a brief introduction and has occasional informative notes introducing passages. There are additional notes at the end of the work and a finding list.

Along with differences in translation style and format, there are also differences in interpretation between the Dobson and the Legge versions. Dobson used the notes of a Han dynasty commentator, while Legge followed the later but more traditional Sung reading. Dobson also had the advantage of being able to make use of the textual and philological research that had been carried out since 1893, when Legge's translation was originally published.

The new translation by D. C. Lau is a long-awaited accomplishment: a translation by the foremost scholar in the West of Chinese philosophy who is at the same time a superb English prose stylist. In Lau's rendition, the arguments are clear and the prose demonstrates that quality that has made the *Mencius* for the Chinese what Luther's translation of the Bible has been for the Germans. The translation is preceded by an illuminating introduction, five appendices (including Lau's article "On Mencius' Use of the Method of Analogy in Argument," *Asia Major*, 1963), textual notes, and a glossary of personal and place names.

52. Watson, Burton, tr. *Basic Writings of Mo Tzu, Hsün Tzu, and Han Fei Tzu.* New York and London: Columbia University Press, 1967. 452 pp.

53. Mo-tzu. *Mo Tzu: Basic Writings.* Tr. by Burton Watson. Paperbound. New York: Columbia University Press, 1963. 140 pp.

54. ———. *The Ethical and Political Works of Motse.* Tr. by Mei Yi-pao. Probsthain's Oriental Series, vol. 19. London: Probsthain, 1929. 275 pp.

55. Hsün-tzu. *Hsün Tzu: Basic Writings.* Tr. by Burton Watson. Paperbound. New York: Columbia University Press, 1963. 177 pp.

56. ———. *The Works of Hsün Tzu.* Tr. by Homer H. Dubs. London: Probsthain, 1928. 336 pp.

57. Dubs, Homer H. *Hsün Tzu: The Moulder of Ancient Confucianism.* London: Probsthain, 1927; Milwaukee: Caspar, Krueger, Dorg, 1930. 308 pp. (Reprinted by Paragon Book Gallery, New York).

58. Han Fei-tzu. *Han Fei Tzu: Basic Writings.* Tr. by Burton Watson. Paperbound. New York: Columbia University Press, 1964. 134 pp.

59. ———. *The Complete Works of Han Fei Tzu.* Tr. by W. K. Liao. 2 vols. Probsthain's Oriental Series, vols. 25 and 26. London: Probsthain, 1939, 1959. 310 and 338 pp.

Translations of important sections from three of the major philosophies of the Warring States period by Burton Watson may be found individually in paperback editions or together in hardback form; the contents are identical. Each highly readable translation also contains a brief but adequate introduction, occasional explanatory notes, and an index. The more complete translations and extensive commentaries of Mei Yi-pao, Homer H. Dubs, and W. K. Liao, are recommended to those readers who, having read the Watson versions, wish to continue their studies. The Watson translations are especially suitable for those primarily interested in Chinese philosophical prose.

The school of Mo Ti or Mo-tzu (ca. 470–391 B.C.), although of importance in the Warring States period, and apparently a rival of Confucianism, has been of little significance in Chinese thought since the Han dynasty. Mo-tzu is noted for his condemnation of offensive warfare and for his doctrine of an artificial universal love, excoriated by the Confucians because it ignored the naturally stronger love between parent and child. His concept of total identification with one's superior in a rigid hierarchical society has also been less than popular. The dry, repetitive prose of the *Mo-tzu* makes it perhaps the least interesting to read of all the major Chinese philosophical works of this period. Burton Watson's translation includes all or parts of eleven chapters ranging from "Universal Love" to "Explaining Ghosts" to "Against Confucius."

The writings of Hsün-tzu (born ca. 312 B.C.) are, along with the *Mencius*, the two most important books of Confucianism following the *Analects*. Although Mencius' interpretation of Confucianism became the orthodox one following the Sung dynasty Neo-Confucianism of Chu Hsi, Hsün-tzu's interpretation may have been the more important through the Han dynasty. The basic difference between the two is their opposite views on human nature. Hsün-tzu viewed man as inherently selfish, hence evil and in need of education to socialize or reform him.

The prose of Hsün-tzu is one of the earliest and finest examples of Chinese expository writing. The title of each chapter expresses the theme of the essay, which is logically developed and includes illustrative quotations from the *Classics of History* and *Poetry*. The style is deliberately literary with balanced rhythmic sentences. The ten chapters translated by Watson include such themes as "Improving Yourself" and "A Discussion of Music."

The book by Han Fei-tzu (d. 233 B.C.), a student of Hsün-tzu, is perhaps *The Prince* (by Machiavelli) of Chinese literature. Han Fei-tzu was himself a prince, the only nobleman among the important early Chinese philosophers. One of his fellow students, Li Ssu (d. 208 B.C.), eventually became the prime minister of the state of Ch'in when it reunited China, instituting the first Chinese empire. While on a mission as envoy to Ch'in from his native state, Han Fei-tzu was put in jail by Li Ssu and there died of poison. His writings, although not the earliest, are the most important of the Legalist or Realist school which promoted a strictly totalitarian government emphasizing law, power, and statecraft. He viewed the strengthening of the state as the sole function of government. Although this work has been theoretically anathema to Chinese thought since the Ch'in dynasty, its brilliant style, if not its lucid arguments on the nature and use of power, has caused it to be read throughout Chinese history. Watson's translation includes twelve chapters from the *Han Fei-tzu* containing, for example, the essays, "Wielding Power" and "The Difficulties of Persuasion."

60. Chuang-tzu. *The Complete Works of Chuang Tzu.* Tr. by Burton Watson. New York: Columbia University Press, 1968. 397 pp.

61. ———. *Chuang Tzu: Basic Writings.* Tr. by Burton Watson. Paperbound. New York: Columbia University Press, 1964. 148 pp.

62. Creel, H. G. "The Great Clod: A Taoist Conception of the Universe." In *Wen-lin: Studies in Chinese Humanities,* ed. by Chow Tse-tsung. pp. 257–268. Madison: University of Wisconsin Press, 1968.

The *Chuang-tzu,* the oldest of the Taoist classics, is considered by some scholars to be the most profound philosophical work ever written; it is at the very least the most delightful. The extant thirty-three-chapter version was edited about A.D. 300 and divided into three parts. The first part, chapters 1–7, probably comprises the earliest strata of the work and clearly is the most important. The Burton Watson translation may be obtained in two versions, a complete hardback one and a shorter paperback version which includes chapters 1–7 plus four of the other more important chapters. Watson's lucid translation, incorporating recent research by Japanese scholars, is by far the best available.

According to the *Shih chi* (no. 35), a man named Chuang-tzu (Master Chuang), whose personal name was Chou, lived in the fourth century B.C. and wrote a book which was "mostly in the nature of a fable." Although the authorship of the various sections of the *Chuang-tzu* is obscure, the oldest strata would approximate this period.

A great number of anecdotes, especially in the first part, interspersed with several types of philosophical arguments, form the *Chuang-tzu.* All of the major philosophers of the period in which the *Chuang-tzu* was written devoted themselves to the problem of man and society in a crumbling world, seeking to reform one or the other or both. According to a personal interpretation, the *Chuang-tzu* views the problem as artificial; a recognition of its artificiality frees the person of this and all problems. Man is but a part of nature, to act otherwise is to contradict his own essence. The only true way to exist is to be completely spontaneous and mindless, becoming as one with the Tao, the totality of everything that is real or natural. Humor and absurdity characterize to a great extent the method of argument adopted in the *Chuang-tzu*.

Although the *Chuang-tzu* is usually enjoyable reading, an understanding of its real meaning requires many readings and much thought. The short article by H. G. Creel may be of some assistance to the first-time reader. Creel contrasts the Western conception of the universe as found in Plato with that of the Taoist. For Plato the truly real is unchanging; for Chuang-tzu, it is in a state of universal flux. The totality of existence, the sum totality of reality is the Tao. A Westerner may "honor the universe by endowing it with human qualities, calling it 'infinite mind' or 'absolute reason.' The Taoist, with an apparent simplicity that is wholly deceptive, with the approach to the ridiculous that always characterizes the sublime, calls it the Great Clod." Watson's translation and interpretation is compatible in that it translates this controversial term in the same way ("Great Clod").

63. Lao-tzu. *Lao tzu: Tao Te Ching*. Tr. by D. C. Lau. Paperbound. Baltimore: Penguin Books, 1963. 191 pp.

64. ———. *Tao Te Ching: The Book of the Way & Its Virtue*. Tr. by J. J. L. Duyvendak. Wisdom of the East Series. London: John Murray, 1954. 172 pp.

65. ———. *The Way and Its Power: A Study of the "Tao Te Ching" and Its Place in Chinese Thought*. Tr. by Arthur Waley. London: George Allen & Unwin; Boston: Houghton Mifflin Co., 1935. 262 pp. (Paperback, Grove Press, Evergreen Book).

66. ———. *The Way of Lao Tzu*. Tr. by Chan Wing-tsit. Indianapolis: Bobbs-Merrill, 1963. 285 pp.

The *Tao te ching* has been translated into European languages more often than any other Chinese work, but these translations differ so greatly that on comparison, many appear to have dissimilar bases. The translation by D. C. Lau offers the best in scholarship and readable English, employing a taut simplicity of language that approaches the original. Other recommended translations are those of Chan Wing-tsit, who is close to D. C. Lau in his interpretation and has included extensive reference aids; J. J. L. Duyvendak, who has attempted to discover the original order for some of the passages; and Arthur Waley, who embodies a fresh approach in his extremely fine rendition with a long introduction that should be most helpful to the layman. The work by D. C. Lau includes an extensive introduction, appendices on "The Problems of Authorship" and "The Nature of the Work," a glossary, and limited textual notes.

According to the tradition found in the *Shih chi* of Ssu-ma Ch'ien (no. 35), Lao-tzu, who was an older contemporary of Confucius and historian in charge of the archives in Chou, left the state when he noted the decline of Chou. As he reached the border, the Keeper of the Pass requested a book; Lao-tzu then wrote the *Tao te ching*. Traditionally the oldest Taoist treatise, the *Tao te ching* is the most important Taoist work. However, the language and philosophy of the work implies a later date, probably the third century B.C., although the author undoubtedly incorporated earlier material. The text, even within the same chapters, is at times contradictory, indicating erratic editing or confusion of the text over time.

The work is brief, divided into eighty-one chapters of a few lines each. Its language is enigmatic, ambiguous and at times hopelessly obscure. The very first line, "The way that can be told/ Is not the constant way," consists of six characters, three of which are identical—*tao*. Although the first line itself has been interpreted in a number of different ways, the above exemplifies the impossibility of communicating, in a direct fashion, the nature of the Tao. "One who knows does not speak; one who speaks does not know." The *Tao te ching* attempts to teach without teaching, to bypass the contradiction through contradiction, to "name" the "nameless." This ambiguity may explain the book's immense popularity in China and increasing interest in the West. It is a little masterpiece of which one does not tire because one's understanding expands with each reading.

67. *Lieh-tzu. The Book of Lieh-tzu.* Tr. by A. C. Graham. The Wisdom of the East Series, vol. 11. London: John Murray, 1950. 183 pp.

The *Lieh-tzu*, the third most important Taoist work, is perhaps the easiest for the Westerner to understand; it contains neither the ambiguity or manifold divergent interpretations of the *Tao te ching,* nor the early formulation of the first part or the philosophical discussion of the latter part of the *Chuang-tzu.* Although tradition ascribes the work to the third century B.C. or earlier (there are early references to a Lieh-tzu who rode on the wind), the *Lieh-tzu* probably dates to the third century A.D., a period of Taoist intellectual ferment. The philosophy of this period, often termed Neo-Taoism by Westerners or *hsüan-hsüeh* ("Subtle Learning") in Chinese, includes the work of some of China's most important and interesting philosophers: Wang Pi (226–249), Hsi K'ang (232–262), and Kuo Hsiang (d. 312) (see section on "Anthologies" for their writings).

The *Lieh-tzu* consists of eight chapters, of which the seventh, "Yang-chu," advocating a hedonistic viewpoint, is decidedly different from the rest. It is unlikely that the original Yang-chu (ca. 350 B.C.), of whom we know very little, advanced this sort of philosophy. The remainder of the work, presented almost entirely in the form of vivid, lively, and often humorous anecdotes (a number from the *Chuang-tzu),* delineates the means of discovering the Way, "a state of heightened perceptiveness and responsiveness in an undifferentiated world."

This lucid and accurate translation by A. C. Graham, a recognized scholar of Chinese literature and philosophy, is the first complete translation in English. The volume contains an introduction which will be especially useful to the general reader, a short reading list, and some textual notes.

68. Hui-neng. *The Platform Scriptures.* Tr. by Chan Wing-tsit. New York: St. John's University Press, 1963. ix, 193 pp.

69. ———. *The Platform Sutra of the Sixth Patriarch.* Tr. by Philip B. Yampolsky. New York: Columbia University Press, 1967. xiv, 216 pp.

The most important text of *Ch'an* ("Zen") Buddhism, the *Plat-*

form Scriptures is the sole Chinese work accorded the title of *sutra* ("scriptures"), normally reserved for texts attributed to the Buddha. The *Platform Scriptures* is a collection of sayings and sermons by Hui-neng, the sixth Ch'an patriarch according to tradition. This work is crucial in the development of Ch'an, as it presents Hui-neng's concept of "sudden enlightenment." This concept was the major point of conflict that resulted in the schism between what came to be known as the Southern School, which supported "sudden enlightenment," and the Northern School, which stressed "gradual enlightenment." Ultimately, the Southern School became the dominant Ch'an tradition:

> It is because people are deluded in their minds and are seeking Buddhahood by external practice, without understanding their own nature, that they are called people of small intelligence. When people hear the doctrine of sudden enlightenment and do not depend on external practice, but simply find correct views in their own nature, all these afflicted are at once enlightened. [Chan, p. 77]

According to the text gathered and recorded by Hui-neng's disciple, Fa-hai, the *Platform Scriptures* was preached by Hui-neng in the Ta-fan Temple in Shao-chou, probably in 677. There is no indication as to whether the sermon was preached in one day or over several days. Some scholars consider the sermon itself (sections 12–37) to be genuine. Other parts of the *Platform Scriptures*, Hui-neng's autobiography (sections 1–11), and the collected sayings and other sermons (sections 38–57) probably include modifications.

Chan's and Yampolsky's translations are based on the Tun-huang manuscript (no. 85, Arthur Waley, *Ballads and Stories from Tun-huang*), which was probably written in the eighth century and was discovered in 1900. The previously known editions, dating to the twelfth and thirteenth centuries, are longer versions. Although the Tun-huang text contains many inaccuracies and was most likely the work of a poorly educated copyist, it is probably the most authentic version known. Hence, if for no other reason than that they are the closest to the original, Chan's and Yampolsky's translations are to be recommended.

Both translations are readily understood, at least superficially, by the general reader and are in general accord with each other, except for minor differences in style, use of Buddhist terminology, and punctuation of the original text. Chan's translation contains a short introduction to the work and the philosophy of Hui-neng, which should be most helpful to the nonspecialist (although it contains some controversial interpretations), and a facing Chinese text, in-text characters, and extensive notes, including variant readings from other texts; all invaluable aids to the specialist. Yampolsky's version contains a lengthy, thorough introduction to the history of Ch'an in the eighth century as well as the text and related legends, a glossary of Chinese characters, a complete bibliography, and the text at the end of the volume. Because of its simpler introduction and easier-to-read format, Chan's edition is recommended for the general reader; the specialist will want both.

70. *The Blue Cliff Records: The Hekigan Roku.* Tr. with extensive commentary by R. D. M. Shaw. London: Michael Joseph, 1961. 229 pp.

Hsüeh-tou Chung-hsien (980–1052), abbot of the temple Ling-ch'uan Yuan, collected a hundred stories and sayings of the *Ch'an* ("Zen") Buddhist tradition to which he appended explanatory verses. Because the abbot's quarters contained a calligraphic scroll of the characters *pi* ("blue/green") and *yen* ("large rock/cliff"), he named the book *Pi yen lu* (Blue Cliff Records, Japanese: Hekigan Roku). Later, Yuan-wu Ko-Ch'in (1063–1135) added an introduction to each of the collection's entries. The work became a minor scripture, provided meditation subjects, and was recited in the temples.

The core ranges from terse, completely enigmatic statements—

Attention! A certain monk asked To-san: What is Buddha? To-san said: Here is hemp—three pounds of it. [p. 61]

to more readily comprehensible stories—

Attention! The Emperor Wu of Ryu (Liang) asked the Bodhisattva Fu to expound to him the Diamond Sutra. The Bodhisattva went up to the dais, sat down on the seat, struck the lectern once with his staff and came down from the dais. The Emperor was dumbfounded. Prince Shi asked him: Your Majesty, have you understood? The Emperor said: I do not understand. Prince Shi said: The Bodhisattva has concluded his exposition of the Scripture. [p. 212]

to stories of several hundreds of words in length. For each selection, R. D. M. Shaw provides a prefatory remark, individual interpretations of the three sections, and commentary and notes. This extensive commentary and interpretation allowed Shaw to translate literally and tersely, the only form of translation that could capture the spirit of even a small part of the original. Ch'an literature is enigmatic and obscure. Ideally it should not exist; as with Taoism, what truly is cannot be expressed in words. Yet were we to accept the advice of Pao-fu (Japanese: Ho-fuku), we would not have this delightful literature:

Cho-kei said: Well, what, then, is the language of the Tathagata [Perfect One—term for the Buddha]? Ho-fuku said: Come, have a cup of tea! [p. 276]

Belles Lettres: Miscellaneous
(Memoirs, Essays, Literary Criticisms)

71. Shen Fu. *Chapters from a Floating Life: The Autobiography of a Chinese Artist.* Tr. by Shirley M. Black. New York: Oxford University Press, 1960. xiv, 108 pp.

Autobiography is uncommon in Chinese literature, yet Shen Fu's masterful description of his life in a more relaxed era ("For a year and a half I was a guest in his home . . .") has universal appeal. A writer and painter, Shen Fu (b. 1783) was fortunate to have a similarly talented and sympathetic wife, Yün, who is, according to Lin Yutang, "one of the loveliest women in Chinese literature." The depiction of their betrothal period, marriage, and life together presents an intimate view of an almost ideal relationship between man and wife in traditional China. The problems of a sensitive artist and his wife in a bureaucratic society and the ensuing poverty and family difficulties provide more poignant reading. Shen Fu ends his memoir four years after Yün's tragic death in 1803.

Aside from the moving story of the author's life, the recordings of the "little pleasures of life" are captivating:

In summer, when the lotus begins to bloom, the flowers fold their petals at night and open them again in the morning. Yuen [Yün] used to put a pinch of tea leaves in a little gauze bag, tuck it in one of the flowers, and leave it there until the next day. When she boiled fresh spring water and made the tea, it had an incomparable fragrance and flavor. [p. 71]

The descriptions of flower arrangement (the section on gardening is unfortunately omitted) and methods of incense burning are both entertaining and instructive.

Shen Fu's autobiography consists of four parts (parts five and six were lost and the present versions of them are spurious): "Wedded Bliss," "The Little Pleasures of Life," "Sorrow," and "The Joys of Travel." The translator included most of the first and third sections, part of the second, and a few incidents from the fourth section, which she rearranged into "a less confusing chronological order." Lin Yutang's complete translation of 1935 may be found in *The Wisdom of China and India* (no. **20**). Mrs.

Black's translation is readable and accurate, but some explanatory notes would have been useful for the general reader. Eight plates, reproducing seventeenth-century paintings which Shen Fu presumably would have admired, are a pleasant addition to this little volume.

72. Kuo Hsi. *An Essay on Landscape Painting.* Tr. by Shio Sakanashi. Wisdom of the East Series. London: John Murray, 1935. 70 pp. (Distr. by Paragon Book Gallery, New York).

Kuo Jo-hsü put the teachings of his father, Kuo Hsi (born ca. 1020), one of the great master-painters of the early Sung dynasty, into its present form and added a preface. The *Lin ch'üan kau chih* (An Essay on Landscape Painting), although not one of the Sung literary masterpieces, is a good example of the balanced prose style, a form of Chinese prose which does not lend itself readily to translation. It is divided into four sections: "Comments on Landscapes," "The Meaning of Painting," "Rules for Painting," and "A Supplement to the Rules for Painting"; the latter, not considered authentic, is not included in the translation.

The essay has been highly influential in the development of Chinese landscape painting and is an invaluable introduction to its appreciation. To the question, "Why does a virtuous man take delight in landscapes," Kuo Hsi explains that since the educated man becomes involved with affairs of the world and is unable to escape civilization, his Taoist nature, his love for the rustic, may find outlet in landscape painting. "Without leaving the room, at once, he finds himself among the streams and ravines; the cries of the birds and monkeys are faintly audible to his senses; light on the hills and reflection on the water, glittering, dazzle his eyes. Does not such a scene satisfy his mind and captivate his heart?" Starting out in this manner, Kuo Hsi proceeds to discuss the different types, approaches, and methods of landscape painting.

73. Williamson, H. R. *Wang An Shih: a Chinese Statesman and Educationalist of the Sung Dynasty.* vol. 2, pp. 264–390. London: Arthur Probsthain, 1935–37.

Wang An-shih (1021–1086) was one of the most important

personages of the Sung dynasty. Appointed Chief Counsellor in 1069, he engendered a number of sweeping reforms to improve the government's financial position and strengthen the army. His reforms were opposed by most of the other great scholar-statesmen of his day, such as Ssu-ma Kuang, Ou-yang Hsiu, and Su Tung-p'o. Because of the many personal animosities he stirred up by his brisk and somewhat crude manner as well as by his reforms, he was forced to resign from office in 1076 and his whole administrative program was reversed.

Aside from his importance in the political sphere, Wang An-shih is famous for his prose and poetry and is considered one of the eight great prose writers (sometimes one of the four best) of the combined T'ang-Sung period. He wrote in a variety of styles and was known by his contemporaries for his originality and spontaneity.

Part of the second volume of H. R. Williamson's two-volume work on Wang An-shih contains translations of many of his essays and discussions of his literary influence. The latter includes three chapters, "The Literature and its History," "Wang An Shih's Contribution to Prose and Poetry," and "Wang An Shih's Contribution to Classical Exposition," which because of their technical nature, may cause difficulties for the general reader.

The twenty-six translated essays are on diverse subjects ranging from philosophy, to educational methodology, to fortune-telling. Although the stylistic qualities of Wang An-shih's prose cannot, of course, be reproduced in translation, Williamson's translations transmit the cogency of Wang An-shih's reasoning and the tautness of his language.

74. Liu Hsieh. *The Literary Mind and the Carving of Dragons: A Study of Thought and Pattern in Chinese Literature.* Tr. with an intro. and notes by Vincent Yu-chung Shih. New York: Columbia University Press, 1959. xlvi, 298 pp.

The second oldest major work on literary criticism after the *Wen fu* (Rhymeprose on Literature) by Lu Chi (261–303) (see *Guide to Chinese Poetry* in this series), and the most thorough, is the *Wen-hsin tiao-lung* (The Literary Mind and the Carving of Dragons) by Liu Hsieh (ca. 456–522). It is a systematic exposition of the techniques of literary composition, written in the parallel prose style, and is itself, like the *Wen fu*, an exemplary work of literature.

The work is divided into fifty essays (of which Vincent Shih translated the first forty-nine; the last deals with miscellaneous topics): the first four are introductory, concerning the nature, origin and purpose of literature; the next twenty-one deal with the various literary forms; and the second half of the work is concerned with the nature and method of literary composition, common flaws, and the method of criticism.

Parallel prose is extremely difficult to render into English, not only because of the style of writing itself, but also because of the great number of literary and historical allusions. The translator has been quite successful in rendering the meaning of the work if not its esthetic qualities. The translation is well annotated and contains an informative introduction, a valuable glossary with the Chinese characters, and an index.

Short Stories

75. Bishop, John Lyman. *The Colloquial Short Story in China: A Study of the "San-yen" Collections.* Harvard-Yenching Institute Studies, vol. 14. Paperbound. Cambridge: Harvard University Press, 1956. 144 pp.

Between 1620 and 1623, three anthologies of 120 short stories by Feng Meng-lung (nos. **93, 94**), collectively known as the *San-yen* ("Three" *Yen*), were published. These collections established the mature short story in the vernacular (in contrast with the short story in the literary or classical language) as a literary genre.

John Bishop, in this excellent study, discusses the stages in the development of colloquial fiction from its origins in the tales of religious and historical legend, through its presentation by storytellers to a relatively lower-class audience, to the gradual evolution of stories written to be read, culminating in the colloquial short-story style of the seventeenth century. Following this introduction, the author analyzes the characteristics of the genre, a combination of fantastic incidents and realistic narrative. Included is a brief comparison of the development of the colloquial short story with the development of early realistic fiction in Europe.

Professor Bishop's study includes translations of four previously untranslated stories each selected "to exemplify a particular type within the genre": detective, love, ghosts and history. The thoroughly annotated translations are complete in every detail and are rendered as close to the original as is compatible with readable English. Thus these translations provide a unique opportunity to understand the method as well as content of the vernacular short story.

Additional reference material includes a complete bibliography of translations of *San-yen* stories into Western languages.

76. Ruhlman, Robert. "Traditional Heroes in Chinese Popular Fiction." In *The Confucian Persuasion*, ed. by Arthur F. Wright. Palo Alto: Stanford University Press, 1960. (Paperback reprint in *Confucianism and Chinese Civilization*, ed.

by Arthur F. Wright. pp. 122–157. New York: Atheneum Publishers, 1964).

Robert Ruhlman has studied the traditional heroes found in Chinese colloquial fiction to augment understanding of Chinese social and intellectual history. Such an approach offers a means, although indirect, of acquiring information usually unavailable on some of the values and attitudes among the common people of China. Of literary benefit is his analysis of the popular and scholarly heroes, a major constituent of Chinese colloquial fiction.

Ruhlman found the heroes to be basically of three types:

the impetuous, uninhibited, and generous Swordsman, a lovable and explosive "good fellow"; the Scholar, of outstanding intelligence, resourcefulness, eloquence, and self-control, "knowing all knowable things and some others," whose powers of reading minds, of seeing into the future, of influencing the forces of nature have a supernatural cast; and the Prince, holder of Heaven's mandate, who does nothing spectacular himself, but is skilled in judging men and in choosing the Scholars and Swordsmen who will enable him to fulfill his destiny. [p. 156]

Because this article was written for a multiple audience, the general reader should find this primarily nontechnical study especially useful.

77. Liu, James J. Y. *The Chinese Knight Errant.* Chicago: University of Chicago Press, 1967. xiv, 242 pp.

Professor Liu traces the rise, social origins, and ideological bases of the behavior of the Chinese knight-errant, providing examples from the various periods of Chinese history. Usually based on historical persons, these legendary warriors and strong men roamed the country using might to right wrong, but as Professor Liu demonstrates, were otherwise quite different from their European counterparts. Following his historical survey, Professor Liu examines the knight-errant as he is found in Chinese poetry, fiction, and drama. A number of the heroes to be found in translated fiction are discussed; for example, the *Curly-Bearded Stranger* and *The K'un-lun Slave* from the T'ang tales, and the heroes of the novel, *Water Margin.* Both general readers and specialists should find the work of interest and value.

78. Bauer, Wolfgang, and Franke, Herbert, trs. *The Golden Casket: Chinese Novellas of Two Millenia.* Tr. from the German version into English by Christopher Levenson. New York: Harcourt, Brace & World, 1964. 391 pp. (Paperback, Penguin).

The Golden Casket, a Chinese term for "Treasure House of Books," is the finest collection of Chinese short stories written in the literary language available in English. This genre of fiction is quite distinct from the short story written in language which to varying degrees approximated speech. Not only is the literary style different, but as the stories were written by the educated for the educated, they often include many literary and historical allusions and poetry.

Bauer and Franke, two notable German sinologists, have translated forty-six of these stories written in the two-thousand-year period from the third century B.C. to the eighteenth century A.D. (although the earliest—narratives from the early historical writings—are not exactly short stories). Included are stories of the classic genre, fictionalized history; tales of the underworld, often of Buddhist influence; stories of swordsmen-heroes, who frequently have magical or supernatural powers; and love stories.

The love stories concern themselves with the classic conflict between arranged marriage and romantic love; courtesans, both golden-hearted and grasping; and affairs with ghosts and were-creatures, especially fox-fairies. Fox-fairies are spirits who, normally found in the shape of foxes, can change themselves into humans, often gifted and beautiful women, and enter into sexual liaisons with men. Sometimes beneficial, these relationships more often meant disaster for the human lover.

Thirty authors are represented, seven by more than one story. Two authors from the Ming dynasty, the most flourishing period of this literary genre, are represented by a number of selections. Ch'ü Yu (ca. 1341–1427), who had a frustrated official career, is the author of five stories. He utilized the short story as a vehicle for social criticism, but also wrote carefree tales of love.

Six stories by Li Ch'ang-chi (1376–1452) are contained in this collection. Successful in his career, he nevertheless suffered serious reverses and wrote on the same themes as Ch'ü Yu.

Because these superior translations were intended for the general reader, they are sometimes freely done. Much of the poetry and allusions which would not be understood without extensive annotations are left out. Such selective editing increases their readability for the nonscholar. Professor Franke has written an informative and helpful introduction, and a list of sources and sparse notes are placed at the end of the work.

79. Waley, Arthur, tr. *Translations from the Chinese*. New York: Alfred A. Knopf, 1941. 325 pp. (Paperback, Vintage Books).

(42.) ———.*The Real Tripitaka and Other Pieces*. London: George Allen & Unwin; New York: Macmillan Co., 1952. 291 pp.

Translations From the Chinese is primarily a collection of poetry, but it does contain two of the longer T'ang dynasty short stories. "The Story of Miss Li" by Po Hsing-chien (799–831), the brother of the famous poet, Po Chü-i, is the same tale as that titled "Story of a Singsong Girl" in *The Dragon King's Daughter* (see no. **87** for plot summary). "The Story of Ts'ui Ying-ying" by Yüan Chen (779–831) is a tale of a broken romance, made up in part by the exchange of letters and notes between the lovers.

The Real Tripitaka and Other Pieces has already been reviewed in a previous entry (no. **42**). This volume includes eight short T'ang dynasty tales and one long eighteenth-century story. As usual, Arthur Waley's translations are highly readable—his work is the standard by which others are judged.

80. Wang Chi-chen, tr. *Traditional Chinese Tales*. (1944). Connecticut: Greenwood Press, 1969. 255 pp.

This collection of twenty Chinese short stories covers most aspects of this genre in China. Two-thirds are written in literary Chinese while the remainder are from colloquial literature. Although nearly half of the stories are selected from the ninth century, those from the sixth to the sixteenth century are included. Each story is on a different subject and the collection covers all of the major short story themes.

The translations, although satisfactory, are often awkward. For example, the first line of "Jenshih, or the Fox Lady" by Shen Chi-chi (750–800) is translated "Jenshih [Miss Jen] was a supernatural creature of the female sex." (Bauer and Franke (see no. **78**) translate this as, "Miss Jen was a female ghost." To be more precise, she was a 'fox fairy.') They lack the grace of free translation, and although faithful to the text, do not have the Chinese flavor of a highly literal translation. No introduction is provided, but there are interesting notes on the authorship and history of the theme for each story at the end of the anthology.

81. Yen, W. W., tr. *Stories of Old China.* Peking: Foreign Languages Press, 1958. 178 pp.

Foreign Languages Press selected for this anthology twenty-two of the forty-one short stories that W. W. Yen (1877–1950) translated into English while under house arrest in Japanese-occupied Hong Kong in 1942. The stories are arranged chronologically, but without any introduction or dates of the respective authors. Six of the stories are from the T'ang dynasty, two each from the Sung and Ming, and the remainder from the Ch'ing dynasty. The translations follow the original closely and on the whole are quite readable except for occasional lapses into awkward English usage. Even without proper editing, this slim volume must be considered a superior collection.

82. Lin Yutang, tr. *Famous Chinese Short Stories.* Paperbound. New York: Pocket Library, 1954. xvii, 299 pp.

All but two of the twenty stories in this collection are from the T'ang and Sung dynasties and are of the literary style. Lin Yutang has arranged them by theme into six groups: "Adventure and Mystery," "Love," "Ghosts," "Juvenile," "Satire" and "Tales of Fancy and Humor." Li Fu-yen (late ninth century) is represented by the largest number of stories, four of the five stories comprising the last group.

Lin Yutang claims to be the narrator of these stories, not their translator. He has used the interesting and valid prerogative of the Chinese storyteller to present the theme in his own fashion to suit the audience. By rewriting the short stories with emphasis on the presentation of typical Chinese themes, Lin Yutang has been successful in widening the potential readership in English. But the reader should be aware that he is not reading Chinese literature in translation. For this purpose he should refer to other collections which contain many of the stories in this anthology. The introduction, as well as presenting the selections, summarizes the history of Chinese short-story writing.

83. Han Ying. *Han shih wai chuan: Han Ying's Illustrations of the Didactic Application of the "Classic of Songs".* Annot. and tr. by James R. Hightower. Harvard-Yenching Institute Monograph Series, vol. 11. Cambridge: Harvard University Press, 1952. vii, 368 pp.

The *Han shih wai chuan* (Exoteric Commentary on the Han School Text of the *Classic of Songs*) is a diverse anthology of ethical, ritual, and anecdotal material attributed to Han Ying (fl. 150 B.C.). Rather than an interpretation of the *Shih ching* (Classic of Songs, see *Guide to Chinese Poetry* in this series), it originally was a textbook demonstrating its practical uses: "a tag to clinch an argument, a stanza to sum up a philosophical principle, a punning line to delight or confuse." Most of the material in the work is of pre-Han dynasty origin. The anecdotal parts, scattered throughout the anthology, although about historical persons and events, are most likely not historical.

The scholarly translation by Professor Hightower is thoroughly annotated. Included in the volume are an introduction, bibliography, finding list, and index with characters.

84. Yang Hsien-yi, and Yang, Gladys, trs. *The Man Who Sold a Ghost: Chinese Tales of the 3rd-6th Centuries.* Peking: Foreign Languages Press, 1958. ix, 162 pp.

The earliest anthologies of "short stories" in China were collections of *chih-kuai* ("tales of the supernatural"). From the end of the Han dynasty to the beginning of the T'ang, Chinese scholars were fascinated by these stories and collected them. Hence, these early short tales are not original compositions, but the recording of an oral tradition. Traces of early Chinese mythology are reflected in the early *chih-kuai*, while a number of the later stories demonstrate Indian Buddhist influence.

The Man Who Sold a Ghost contains eighty stories from eighteen collections of tales of the supernatural, dating from the third to sixth centuries. They are usually short and written as an account of a strange but factual incident, more in the style of journalism than fiction.

North of the market are two lanes called Tzuhsiao and Fengchung, where live the coffin-makers and undertakers. Sun Yen, a professional mourner, married a woman who went to bed fully dressed. She did this for three years, till Sun's curiosity was aroused. One night he undressed her while she was asleep—and found a furry tail three feet long like a fox's brush! Sun was afraid and divorced her; but when leaving she seized a knife, cut off his hair and ran. When the neighbours pursued her she turned into a fox and they could not catch up with her. After this more than a hundred and thirty citizens in the capital lost their hair. The fox would change into a smart, well-dressed woman, and when passers-by were attracted and drew near she would cut off their hair. So any gaily-dressed woman in those days was pointed at as a fox-fairy. This happened in the fourth month of the second year of the Hsiping period (517), but that same autumn these disturbances stopped. [p. 131]

Others are anecdotal in form:

In the third year of the Taming period (459) a man named Wang Yao died of illness in the capital of the kingdom of Sung. After his death the house was haunted by a lean, swarthy ghost bare from the waist up, wearing nothing but a pair of breeches. This ghost used to sing, shout and imitate men's speech, and often threw filth in their food. Then it moved on to some neighbours named Yu on the east, and made the same trouble there.

Yu said to the ghost: "I don't mind you throwing mud and stones at me. If you were to throw money, I really should be put out."

Then the ghost threw several dozen new coins at him, hitting him on the forehead.

"These small, new coins are not so bad," said Yu. "It's the older ones that I'm afraid of."

Then the ghost threw old coins at him. This happened six or seven times, till Yu had more than one hundred coins altogether. [p. 121]

This edition has a short, informative foreword discussing

the style of the genre as well as its Chinese Communist ideological import. There are four plates and an appendix with notes on the collections from which the stories were taken.

85. Waley, Arthur, tr. *Ballads and Stories from Tun-Huang*. New York: The Macmillan Co., 1960. 273 pp.

At Tun-huang in the extreme northwest of China in 1900, a Taoist, an ex-soldier named Wang Yüan-lu, discovered a walled-up library in the cave in which he was residing. Within a dozen years the documents, dating from A.D. 406 to 996, gathered by foreign scholars, were scattered in London, Paris, Peking, and Japan. This volume of translations by Arthur Waley deals with specimens of popular literature found in that cave: ballads, stories, and legendary expansions and expositions of Buddhist scriptures.

There are fifteen translated secular and sacred prose stories among the twenty-six translated pieces, the majority being popular fiction of the *pien-wen* type (see introduction, p. 13). These highly readable translations designed for the general reader embody a tremendous amount of scholarship, providing both the specialist and general reader an opportunity to attain some familiarity with one of the most important developments of twentieth-century Chinese studies. However, due to the fragmentary condition of the texts, the alternations of prose and rhymed verse, the sometimes primitive nature of the fiction, and peripheral knowledge of Chinese required for a fuller understanding of the early pieces, the general reader may find these stories somewhat less than satisfying.

Aside from the excellent and valuable translations, the two afterwords and five appendices, especially "The Discovery and Nature of the Manuscript" and "The Meaning of Pien-wen and Fu," are recommended. The volume ends with fifteen pages of translation notes and an index.

86. Chang Wen-ch'eng. *The Dwelling of Playful Goddesses: China's First Novelette*. Annot. and tr. by Howard S. Levy. Tokyo: Dai Nippon Insatsu, 1965. iii, 119 pp. (Distr. by Paragon Book Gallery, New York).

The *Yu hsien k'u* (Journey to the Abode of the Fairies or Dwelling of the Playful Goddesses) may be the first fully developed Chinese novelette. Ascribed to Chang Wen-ch'eng (ca. 657–730), this pioneering work, blending poetry and parallel prose, preserves the colloquial idiom of its time. The theme is not original: a young scholar-official discovers two beautiful fairies dwelling in a lonely secluded mountain setting; from the first meeting, through dinner and entertainment, the emotional and erotic tension builds, leading to the climactic bedroom scene. The original version to this in a far simpler and shorter form is probably the *Mei-jen fu* (Ode on a Beautiful Woman), a *fu* ("prose-poem") by the great Han poet Ssu-ma Hsiang-ju (179–117 B.C.) (see no. **10**, pp. 108–9 for partial translation). It is Chang Wen-ch'eng's exquisite handling of this theme that marks its literary merit. The story is also the first important erotic Chinese work and may have influenced attitudes toward love in subsequent Chinese fiction.

Levy has succeeded in preserving many of the esthetic qualities of the original. But the number of historical and literary allusions (the translation is fully annotated), and the difficulties of rendering parallel prose and the extensive verse dialogue into English, may pose problems for the general reader. The translation comprises only half of the volume; there are also essays on the form and content, authorship and text of the work, as well as on its influence on Japanese literature. The text was lost in China soon after its compilation, but was preserved in Japan where, according to Levy, it exerted a wide influence on the development of Japanese literature. Appended to the volume is an extensive, annotated bibliography.

87. Yang Hsien-yi, and Yang, Gladys, trs. *The Dragon King's Daughter: Ten T'ang Dynasty Stories*. 2d rev. ed. Peking: Foreign Languages Press, 1962. x, 99 pp.

During the T'ang dynasty, the short story evolved from the recording of oral folktales into a form of creative writing. Although some authors continued to end their narrative with the traditional description of the circumstances under which the story was recorded, these tales nevertheless can be classified as creative literature. The stories were written in the literary language in a refined and polished style. They, together with poetry, were the highest literary attainments of this period.

Tales of the supernatural continue from the Six Dynasties period as the most popular type of story: themes revolve around ghosts, deities, were-animals, dreams in which men live entire lives within a span of a few hours and are consequently led to adopt the Taoist hermit's life. More than half the stories center on love, some involving relationships with supernatural beings. Other popular themes encompass heroes with magical powers and legends concerning historical figures.

The Dragon King's Daughter is a representative collection of ten T'ang dynasty short stories. Eight of these tales can be found in other collections listed in this section of our bibliography, but this anthology is a slim, attractive, compact volume in the same format as *The Man Who Sold a Ghost.*

All of the above-mentioned themes are included in the collection. Of interest is the development of the romance theme separate from the tale of the supernatural. It is but a single step from a ghost or were-fox lover to a human one. In the "Story of a Singsong Girl," the son of a governor, away from home to take the provincial examination, takes a courtesan as a mistress. After living with her for a year, he becomes penniless from wasting his fortune on her and is tricked into leaving. He suffers every kind of degradation, even an almost fatal beating by his father for being a worthless son. As a filthy, diseased, emaciated beggar, one day he comes across his former lover who, ashamed because she has reduced him to this pathetic condition, purchases her freedom, nurses him back to health, and supports, encourages, and guides his studies. He eventually achieves high distinction in the examinations and is given an official position. His new superior turns out to be his father, who forgives him and insists he marry the girl, even though she is of lowly status.

The English translations have been improved upon in the revised edition. The volume contains an introduction, five plates taken from late sixteenth- or seventeenth-century editions of plays based on the T'ang dynasty stories, and a map of the T'ang dynasty capital, Ch'ang-an, marking the location of six of the stories.

88. Wang, Elizabeth Te-chen, tr. *Ladies of the T'ang: 22 Classical Chinese Stories*. Taipei: Heritage Press, 1961. xi, 347 pp.

Many of the twenty-two stories from the T'ang period translated in this volume can be found in better translations in the preceding entries, but this is the largest collection of the developed T'ang story available in a popular edition. The title is deceptive, for the collection is a representative assortment of the best of the various types of T'ang short stories in the classical language. All but one of the tales were taken from the *T'ai-p'ing kuang-chi*, a Sung dynasty encyclopedic collection of writings from the T'ang dynasty and earlier, one of the major sources for pre-Sung fiction.

The translations, though quite readable, are overly literal, with occasional poor usage of English idiom and a paucity of notes and explanatory material. The introduction presents a brief history of Chinese fiction to the T'ang period and each story is provided with a short preface. The prefaces are of special interest, for not only are the authors and themes discussed, but the later occurrence of similar plots in novels and drama is reviewed.

89. P'u Sung-ling. *Strange Stories from a Chinese Studio*. Tr. and annot. by Herbert A. Giles. (1908, 1916 in 2 vols.). 3d ed. rev. New York: Boni & Liveright, 1925. 488 pp. (Paperback, Dover Publications).

90. ———. *Chinese Ghost and Love Stories*. Tr. by Rose Quong. New York: Pantheon Books, 1946. 329 pp.

We know very little about the life of P'u Sung-ling (1640–1715), called Liu-hsien (Last of the Immortals) by his friends, save that, unsuccessful in the examinations and hence unable to follow the usual career of the educated as a government official, he devoted himself to collecting folk tales. His anthology, *Liao-chai chih-i* (Strange Stories from the Refuge of My Study) was completed in 1679, but was passed around in manuscript form and not printed until 1740.

The stories gathered by P'u Sung-ling were rewritten in the terse literary style, as were the anthologies in the T'ang dynasty, and are the finest examples of the genre. Therefore, unlike the vernacular stories such as those edited by Feng Meng-lung, their readership was limited to the educated class. The themes are also similar to those of the T'ang period and, as the title indicates, are concerned with strange and supernatural events: singing frogs, sea monsters, unusual weather, rare diseases, travel in strange lands, magic, alchemy, etc.

Herbert Giles translated 164 of the approximately four hundred stories in the *Liao-chai,* leaving out those stories that were repetitious and others he considered vulgar (from the Victorian standpoint). The translations are literal and yet, except for occasional use of Victorian idioms, highly readable and well annotated. Professor Giles's introduction includes a complete translation of the author's own record of his life, written on the completion of his anthology. As an appendix, Giles added a translation of the *Yü li ch'ao chuan* (Divine Panorama), a description of the Ten Courts of Justice of the popular Taoist purgatory.

The translations by Rose Quong consist of forty of the longer *Liao-chai* stories. They are similar to Herbert Giles's translations but are of a more contemporary idiom, although they lack the latter's scholarly and helpful annotations. This volume contains a short introduction by Martin Buber (taken from his own German translation of several stories from the *Liao-chai* published in 1911), a few sparse notes at the end of the work, and a number of reproduced illustrations.

91. Soulié de Morant, George, tr. *Chinese Love Tales.* Garden City, New Jersey: Halcyson House, 1935. 161 pp. (Previously published as "Eastern Shame Girl").

All of the seven seventeenth-century Chinese short stories in this volume concentrate on the theme of love. The first, given the unfortunate title of "Eastern Shame Girl" (original title: "Tu Shih-niang in Anger Sinks the Jewel-box") by the translator, uses a plot that was very popular at the height of Chinese romanticism. A young man, sent to the capital to study for the examination by his father, an official, falls in love with a young, well-known courtesan. The girl returns his love and he, having wasted all of his funds at the brothel, manages to borrow enough money to purchase her. On the way back to his home by barge, fearing his father's wrath at his wasted time and money and knowing that his love will certainly be considered unsuitable, he falls in with a wealthy libertine who convinces him to sell the girl for a large sum. When he approaches the girl with this proposition—the evidence of his weak character—she coolly acquiesces and after the transaction takes place, shows him a fortune in jewelry she has been secretly carrying with her to appease his father. Heartbroken, she jumps overboard with the coffer of jewels.

These love stories often concern adolescent boys and girls in conflict between traditionally arranged marriage and love, often unsought, for another. Because of their youth, the love between the two is usually of childlike simplicity and purity. A good example is "A Complicated Marriage." A marriage is about to take place between a couple betrothed by their parents, when the young man becomes ill. Fearing to marry their daughter to someone who might soon die (widows from good families were expected not to remarry), and unable to postpone the arrangements, the parents send their son dressed as a girl in their daughter's place. Because the young man is too ill to receive his supposed bride and so she would not be lonely in her new home, the husband's sister is sent to sleep with the new "bride." The two find themselves becoming fast friends, and as the boy gently reveals his true identity, their friendship deepens into love. Since both are already betrothed, a magistrate is required to rearrange the various betrothals so that morality, love, and propriety are all satisfied.

Other stories in this volume deal with the humorous: a very young man with an enormous appetite is marooned under the bed of a young girl on her family's barge; a lecher disguises himself as a sewing woman and has remarkable success as a seducer until finally caught; the monks of a monastery famed for curing sterility resort to physical rather than spiritual aid.

The translations in this volume, perhaps because of being flawed by stronger adherence to the Chinese than is often preferred, maintain the naive charm of the original stories. There is no introductory material.

92. Yen Tun-yi, ed. *The Courtesan's Jewel Box: Chinese Stories of the Xth-XVIIth Centuries.* Tr. by Yang Hsien-yi and Gladys Yang. Peking: Foreign Languages Press, 1957. 553 pp.

This volume is the largest collection of vernacular short stories available in English. Five of the twenty stories may be dated from the Sung dynasty; the remainder are from the Ming. The stories were chosen from the collections edited by Feng Meng-lung and Lin Meng-chu, both of the early seventeenth century. Many are of novella length—the longest, "The Oil Vendor and the Courtesan," translates to over fifty pages. The plots are complex, and the personalities of the protagonists are relatively well developed. By way of introduction, stories are often preceded by another short story on the same theme. Written in the vernacular, and often from the standpoint of the common people, the stories present a more complete and accurate view of Chinese society than the stories in the literary language.

The plots are many and diverse but, more often than not, center on aspects of love. The story from which the title of the collection was taken, "The Courtesan's Jewel Box," is the same story as "Eastern Shame Girl," the original title story of *Chinese Love Tales* (no. 91). Stories not infrequently have surprise endings. For example, when two devoted brothers, both adopted a few years before by a virtuous couple, now deceased, reach the age of marriage, one reveals herself to be a young woman who had never found the opportunity to rid herself of the disguise she had assumed to protect herself while traveling; and the "brothers" become husband and wife.

The stories were rewritten in the Ming dynasty to illustrate moral behavior and all reflect this orientation to varying degrees. An orphaned and penniless young scholar considers himself fortunate to be able to marry the daughter of a wealthy beggar-chief. Beautiful and intelligent, she encourages and aids him in his studies so that he succeeds to an official career at an early age. Then, ashamed of his wife's social background, he attempts to drown her, leaving her for dead. She is saved and adopted by one of his superiors, and through an intermediary, this official offers his new daughter in marriage to the young man, who readily accepts. After his utter embarrassment upon discovering who his new wife is, and after her not unexpected fit of fury, the couple become reconciled.

Variations on ghost stories are still a favorite. In one story, a young man does not fall prey to a woman's charms; this is to his good fortune for she turns out to be a ghost who had become enamored of him before she had died. A love tale with a twist at the end tells of a man who fatally discovers that his wife had been killed years before; it was her ghost, as well as the ghosts of her parents, with whom he had been living. These two and the story of the revenge of were-foxes on a cruel youth are typical T'ang dynasty themes.

Stories of corruption and honest officials can be viewed as social criticism; an honest official destroyed by a powerful but thoroughly corrupt family is revenged by his son. There is the tale of a secret will and an intelligent if somewhat self-serving magistrate and, in another story, a young man is repeatedly duped by fake alchemists.

The English translations are literal and faithful to the original except for the exclusion of introductory passages requiring extensive commentary and some poetry. The often awkward English usage is not an obstacle to one's enjoyment of these renditions. However, the unfortunate practice of translating Chinese poetry into rhymed English verse was followed. Unless employed by a highly talented writer, this method destroys all of the Chinese esthetic qualities; the translated poem usually reads like doggerel. There is a brief but adequate introduction by the editor. Twenty-two full-plate illustrations reproduced from early seventeenth-century editions of these stories enhance this attractive publication.

93. Feng Meng-lung. *Four Cautionary Tales.* Tr. by Harold Acton and Lee Yi-hsieh. London: John Lehmann, 1947. 159 pp.

94. ———. *Stories from a Ming Collection: The Art of the Chinese Story-teller.* Tr. with commentary by Cyril Birch (1959). New York: Grove Press, 1968. 205 pp. (Paperback).

Feng Meng-lung (1574–1646) was a scholar-official with an interest in the lighter aspects of literature. His diverse compositions include plays, poems, anthologies of short stories, accounts of contemporary events, and handbooks on games. In editing his anthologies, the *San-yen* (see no. **75**), he collected many storyteller's promptbooks *(hua-pen)*, especially of the Southern Sung, and rewrote them to varying extents, possibly adding some original stories of his own. Feng Meng-lung's anthologies embody the finest examples of the Chinese vernacular short story.

Four Cautionary Tales are translations from Feng Meng-lung's anthology, *Hsing-shih heng-yen* (Common Tales to Rouse the World), published in 1627. The title of Acton and Lee's volume of four translated stories reflects the moralistic veneer applied to many of the vernacular stories edited or written in the seventeenth century. Two of the four stories are available in other translations: "Love in a Junk" in Soulié de Morant's *Chinese Love Tales* and "Brother or Bride?" in *The Courtesan's Jewel Box* as "The Two Brothers" (see nos. **91**, **92** for plot summaries). "The Everlasting Couple" is a story of a marriage accentuating Confucian morality rather than love; "The Mandarin-Duck Girdle" involves a missing husband and son (of different families), men disguised as nuns in bawdy convents, suspected murder and misidentified bodies. The translations are among the best to be found of Chinese short stories and include the introductory short stories, which are in italics. This little volume is preceded by an excellent introduction by Arthur Waley, and concludes with selected explanatory notes to the stories.

Stories From a Ming Collection contains six stories from Feng Meng-lung's *Ku-chin hsiao-shuo* (Stories Old and New), the first of his *San-yen* collections. Professor Birch has prepared unabridged translations, the only ones available, in order to present "the art of the Chinese story-teller." All of the conventions are left in: the poetry, occasionally extensive; the sometimes multiple introductory tales; the words and admonitions of the storyteller to the audience. The reader is left with the impression of actually hearing the story being told and perhaps can imagine himself sitting in an open-air Chinese market with the rest of the listeners.

One story, "The Lady Who Was a Beggar," may also be found translated in a less complete version in *The Courtesan's Jewel*

Box as "The Beggar Chief's Daughter" (no. **92**). "The Journey of the Corpse," one of the two tales that involve legendary accounts of historical persons, is presented in a most interesting fashion. Professor Birch first translated a literary version by Niu Su (active ca. 804), then the Ming vernacular version. By comparing the two, one can observe some of the developments which had taken place in the art of Chinese fiction.

The "Pearl-sewn Shirt," the longest story in Feng Meng-lung's collection, translates to over fifty pages. Its many twists and turns concerning broken and re-formed marriages are too complex to summarize, but the story's deep penetration into the tragedy of a broken marriage shows obvious literary maturity. One can view the characters in the story as human beings caught up in events not of their own making.

Other stories include the familiar supernatural theme, here concerned with Taoist "immortals," and an early example of the "detective" story. These detective stories are different from those in the West as the crime is described in the beginning of the story and the plot involves the efforts of the clever magistrate to discover and apprehend the criminal. In "The Canary Murders," the magistrate plays a small role; here the crime is solved by friends of the man wrongly executed for the original crime.

Cyril Birch's translations of the vernacular short story are undoubtedly the finest; even the poetry is clear and enjoyable. Besides an introduction to the volume, each story is preceded by additional informative commentary, often extensive. Complete annotations are placed at the end of the volume.

Novels

95. Hsia, C. T. *The Classic Chinese Novel: A Critical Introduction.* New York: Columbia University Press, 1968. xi, 413 pp. (Paperback).

Readers of Chinese novels in translation are usually handicapped by a number of problems—abridged or expurgated translations, ignorance of the cultural and literary milieu, etc.—which often serve to cause misunderstandings and lack of appreciation. This work by one of the foremost scholars of the Chinese novel will eliminate many of these difficulties. Following an excellent introduction to the Chinese novel, C. T. Hsia discusses the six historically most important Chinese novels, devoting forty to fifty pages to each: *The Romance of the Three Kingdoms, The Water Margin, Journey to the West, Chin P'ing Mei, The Scholars,* and *Dream of the Red Chamber.* All of these works are available in translation (see specific citations).

Because Chinese novels naturally reflect the often radically different culture of China, they are especially difficult for the Western reader to understand. C. T. Hsia has examined these novels from both the Chinese and the Western approaches to literature. The combination of these approaches has led to invaluable insights which will enable the Western reader to enjoy the literary merit of these novels. The essays are oriented toward a multi-audience: the general reader, teachers and students, and specialists in Chinese literature. The latter will find the textual discussions, notes, and bibliography most useful. A reading of the appropriate section of this work is especially recommended before reading a translation of a Chinese novel.

96. Feuerwerker, Yi-tse Mei. "The Chinese Novel." In *Approaches to the Oriental Classics: Asian Literature and Thought in General Education,* ed. by William Theodore de Bary. pp. 171–185. New York: Columbia University Press, 1959.

"The Chinese Novel " is one of a series of papers originally presented at the "Conference on Oriental Classics in General Education" held at Columbia University in 1958. Feuerwerker discusses the novel focusing on its use in college-level general education courses. In the space of a short article, she deals with the development and place of the novel in Chinese literature and ways in which the novel may be approached, and she gives her attention to three of China's most important novels, all readily available in translation: *Journey to the West, Chin P'ing Mei* and *Dream of the Red Chamber.* This article is recommended as the minimal introductory work for a more complete appreciation of a Chinese novel.

97. Buck, Pearl S. *The Chinese Novel.* New York: John Day Co., 1939. 59 pp.

"The Chinese Novel" is the Nobel Lecture delivered by Pearl Buck before the Swedish Academy at Stockholm, December 12, 1938. She was awarded the Nobel Prize for Literature "for rich and genuine epic portrayals of Chinese and peasant life, and for masterpieces of biography." To Pearl Buck, "it is the Chinese and not the American novel which has shaped [her] own effort in writing." In her lecture, she discusses the development, nature, and significance of the Chinese novel.

She views the novel in China as always widely separated from art, art being the exclusive property of the scholars who ignored the people, who in turn laughed at the scholars. According to her, the scholars did not consider the novel as literature and ostentatiously ignored it: the novel was the peculiar product of the common people, written for their own amusement in their own language. Mrs. Buck points out that the origin of the novel is in the recording of professional storytellers' tales and observes that the authors of the final forms of the novels were lost in obscurity, partly because scholars under assumed names did for various reasons write novels in the same simple and natural style. Mrs. Buck considers China's three great novels to be the *Shui hu chuan* (Water Margin), *San-kuo* (Romance of the Three Kingdoms) and *Hung lou meng* (Dream of the Red Chamber) and discusses each in detail as well as others to a lesser extent.

The Chinese Novel is an excellent, brief, general introduction to the Chinese novel, although Mrs. Buck's heavy emphasis on the novel as folk literature would not be universally accepted. The novels were in fact written or rewritten by scholars and enjoyed by them, although not always openly, and the recording and editing of folk tales was considered a valid avocation. China's greatest and perhaps most popular novel, the *Hung lou meng*, is a semi-autobiographical novel by a known author written in a refined colloquial style incorporating poetry in the literary language.

98. Lo Kuan-chung. *Romance of the Three Kingdoms (San Kuo Chih Yen-i)*. Tr. by C. H. Brewitt-Taylor. 2 vols. (1925). Rutland, Vermont: Charles E. Tuttle Co., 1959. xviii, 638 and viii, 623 pp.

The *San-kuo chih yen-i* (Romance of the Three Kingdoms) is the oldest Chinese novel available in translation and the best example of Chinese fictionalized history. More closely based on authentic personalities and events than later historical romances, the novel is in a sense a popularization of Ch'en Shou's *San-kuo chih* (Annals of the Three Kingdoms) and its commentaries, a history covering one of the most popular periods in Chinese history. The *San-kuo* ("Three Kingdoms") period (A.D. 220–265) covers the period from the end of the Han, China's first great dynasty; through its dissolution and division into the three kingdoms Wei, Wu, and Shu; to the brief unification of China. This was the age of famous heroes, villains and battles, the stuff of historical folklore and of the Yüan dynasty *p'ing-hua*, a series of popular historical narratives of the storytellers.

There is a paucity of research on the authorship of the novel. Lo Kuan-chung (ca. 1330–1400), of whom little is known, wrote a unified, relatively factual account of the Three Kingdoms period in the popular literary form. The standard text is the one edited by the father-and-son team, Mao Lun and Mao Tsung-kang of the seventeenth century, who added more of the novelistic conventions; for example, the words, "Empires wax and wane; states cleave asunder and coalesce," that open and close the 120 chapters.

The vast scope of the novel with its wealth of detail precludes any summary of the work. Of the hundreds who march across its pages, it primarily focuses on several personages whose personalities and characters become well defined through the carefully constructed narrative. In the novel these heroes of epic proportions, generals and their retainers, strive for the ultimate political authority. Roy A. Miller in his introduction to the translation says that it is "a fascinating novel whose chief theme is the nature of human ambition."

The relatively complete translation by Brewitt-Taylor is a tour de force of over twelve hundred smoothly translated pages. (There are, however, errors, inevitable in any translation of this length.) But, this mammoth tale, based as it is on Chinese popular history, is likely to overwhelm the general reader. The short but informative introduction written for the 1959 edition by Roy A. Miller is a valuable aid, but it is hoped that future editions will supply character lists and chapter summaries.

99. Shih Nai-an. *All Men are Brothers (Shui hu chuan).* Tr. by Pearl S. Buck. 2 vols. New York: John Day Co., 1933. xiv, 1279 pp. (Reprinted by Grove Press, New York, 1957; several other reprint editions available).

100. ———. *Water Margin.* Tr. by J. A. Jackson. (2 vols., 1937). 2 vols. in 1. New York: Paragon Book Gallery, 1968. 917 pp. (Paperback).

101. Irwin, Richard Gregg. *The Evolution of a Chinese Novel: Shui-hu-chuan.* Harvard-Yenching Institute Studies, vol. 10. Cambridge: Harvard University Press, 1953. ix, 231 pp.

102. Hsia, C. T. "Comparative Approaches to *Water Margin.*" *Yearbook of Contemporary and General Literature,* 11 (1962): 121–128. Bloomington: Indiana University Press.

The *Shui hu chuan* (Water Margin) is the finest example of the Chinese "hero" novel, an episodic form based on the fictional and fictionalized exploits of historic incidents. Shui-hu refers to a marshy area which served as the headquarters for a band of 108 brigand-heroes, each treated by the novelist as a distinct individual. Although rebels, they are revolting against corrupt officials rather than against the government itself. The episodes have a historical basis. A band of thirty-six outlaws, including the hero, Sung Chiang, were active from about 1117 to 1121, just prior to the collapse of the Northern Sung period.

The history of the existing text is rather complex. These popular stories were first written down in the storyteller's prompt-books and were eventually strung together. In the Yüan dynasty, the stories were dramatized on the stage. The authorship of the novel is traditionally ascribed to Shih Nai-an whose version was the primary source for the more fully developed version by Lo Kuan-chung (the assumed author of the *San-kuo chi yen-i*, no. 98). With some cutting and additional material, a version of 100 chapters was later produced about 1550. In the early seventeenth century, a further expanded version of 120 chapters appeared. Finally, in 1644, a shortened edition of 70 chapters with a new conclusion that avoided lauding the brigands as heroes in an unjust era appeared and supplanted the other version in popularity. It is this version that has been translated into English.

Each of the English translations has its merits and disadvantages. Pearl Buck's smooth literal translation with some expurgation is quite faithful to the text. Mr. Jackson's somewhat condensed translation utilizes paraphrase to a much greater extent, but he has maintained the feeling of action and rapid movement lacking in Mrs. Buck's treatment. Considering the length of the novel, it is not surprising that there are a great many inaccuracies in both versions. Mrs. Buck begins with a brief introduction while Mr. Jackson provides a helpful list of the 108 heroes and other characters giving their names, "nicknames," and the chapters in which they first appear. The title of Mrs. Buck's translation, *All Men are Brothers,* is derived from an often-repeated phrase in the novel from the *Analects* of Confucius: "Between the four seas, all men are brothers."

The monograph by Richard Irwin, *The Evolution of a Chinese Novel,* is a comprehensive treatment of the *Shui hu chuan.* Professor Irwin presents a thorough scholarly analysis of the historical foundations and evolution of the novel that serves as a case study of the development of the episodic novel form. As an appendix, he provides several research aids including a chapter-by-chapter summary of the 120-chapter edition of the novel.

C. T. Hsia, in his article, "Comparative Approaches to *Water Margin*," discusses both the weak and strong points of the novel, comparing it with Western literature. In relating the *Water Margin* to the tradition of the popular historical chronicles, Professor Hsia accounts "for its long stretches of dull narrative" in terms of 'pseudo-history'. He also examines the moral and psychological aspects of the novel, emphasizing "its gang morality and mysogyny."

103. Wu Ch'eng-en. *Monkey*. Tr. by Arthur Waley. London: George Allen & Unwin, 1942. 305 pp. (Reprinted by John Day, New York, 1944; Grove Press, Evergreen Books, New York, 1958; and Penguin Books, Harmondsworth, 1961).

104. Hsia, C. T., and Hsia, T. A. "New Perspectives on Two Ming Novels: *Hsi yu chi* and *Hsi yu pu*." In *Wen-lin*, ed. by Chow Tse-tsung. pp. 229–246. Madison: University of Wisconsin Press, 1968.

105. Dudbridge, Glen. *The "Hsi-yu chi": A Study of Antecedents to the Sixteenth-Century Chinese Novel*. Cambridge: At the University Press. 1970. 219 pp.

The *Hsi yu chi* (Record of a Journey to the West) is the foremost example of the novel on a supernatural theme. Theoretically, it is based on the travels of Hsüan-tsang, a Chinese Buddhist monk with the religious name San-tsang (or Tripitaka—the collection of Buddhist scripture), who traveled to India and was away from China for seventeen years (629–645). Having left China surreptitiously, as his request to make the journey had been denied, he became a noted Sanskrit and Buddhist scholar in India, returned to China a national hero, became a favorite of the Emperor, and was extremely influential in the development of Chinese Buddhism. Hsüan-tsang wrote an account of his travels, describing the many difficulties he encountered at the start of his journey. These became popular subjects for the storytellers, and many Indian and Chinese supernatural themes merged into the tales. In the Yüan dynasty they served as the subject for drama.

Wu Ch'eng-en (ca. 1506–82) is generally agreed to be the author of a work of 100 chapters entitled *Hsi yu chi*, which brought the material together in the form of a novel. By this time the story had little relation to the original Tripitaka, who in the novel is a mythical hero, a potential bodhisattva and a comic figure—"Tripitaka stands for the ordinary man, blundering anxiously through the difficulties of life" (Waley, *Monkey*). The real hero of the novel is Monkey, a supernatural animal hatched from a stone egg, a genius with an erratic and mischeivous flair, who to redeem himself for past misdeeds, is sent to aid Tripitaka in his quest for holy scriptures. Two others are companions of Tripitaka in this seriocomic allegory: Pigsy, symbolizing the gross physical appetites, and Sandy, a less colorful figure.

Monkey is unique in its combination of beauty with absurdity, of profundity with nonsense. Folk-lore, allegory, religion, history, antibureaucratic satire and pure poetry—such are the singularly diverse elements out of which the book is compounded. [Waley, p. 9]

As the novel is episodic in nature, rather than condense the work, Arthur Waley, in his superb partial translation, translated thirty chapters nearly in full. *The Real Tripitaka* (no. **42**) is his biography of the historical Hsüan-tsang. The first half of C. T. Hsia's article, "Monstrous Appetite: Comedy and Myth in the *Hsi yu chi*" (pp. 229–239) in "New Perspectives on Two Ming Novels," distinguishes two types of comedy in the mythical aspect of the novel: political satire and "an oblique religious commentary exposing the falsity of appearance and the absurdity of man's inordinate appetite." Glen Dudbridge's work, *The Hsi-yu chi*, is a technical examination of the various origins of the novel, including a study of apes and monkeys in Chinese literature.

106. *Chin P'ing Mei. The Golden Lotus.* Tr. by Clement Egerton. 4 vols. London: Routledge and Kegan Paul, 1939; New York: Grove Press, 1954. xix, 387; vii, 376; vii, 385; and vii, 375 pp.

107. ———. *Chin P'ing Mei: The Adventurous History of Hsi Men and His Six Wives.* Tr. by Bernard Miall from the German version by Franz Kuhn. (1940 in 2 vols.). 2 vols. in 1. New York: G. P. Putnam & Sons, 1947. xxii, 863 pp. (Paperback).

108. Hanan, P. D. "A Landmark of the Chinese Novel." In *The Far East: China & Japan,* ed. by Douglas Grant and Miller MacLure, pp. 325–335. University of Toronto Quarterly Supplements. Toronto: University of Toronto Press, 1961.

109. *Ko-lien hua-ying. Flower Shadows Behind the Curtain: A Sequel to "Chin P'ing Mei."* Tr. by Vladimir Kean from the German version by Franz Kuhn. New York: Pantheon Books; London: Bodley Head, 1959. 432 pp.

The authorship of the *Chin P'ing Mei* (the title refers to three of the women involved in the novel), written in the first half of the sixteenth century, is still controversial. Arthur Waley, in his introduction to Bernard Miall's translation, suggests the important playwright Hsü Wei (1521–93) as the author. According to one legend, Wang Shih-chen (1526–90), a notable poet and prose writer, wrote the novel to avenge his father's death, which had been caused by the minister Yen Shih-an. Wang coated the page corners of the manuscript with poison. Fond of pornography, Yen Shih-an read the work through at one sitting; as he licked his finger to turn the pages, he accumulated enough poison in his system to die the instant he finished the novel.

The *Chin P'ing Mei* is undoubtedly erotic, perhaps pornographic, but the novel is primarily concerned with social and cultural change, as Patrick Hanan in "A Landmark in the Chinese Novel" points out: "There are two questions in which the *Chin P'ing Mei* is saturated; money and social status." The plot of the novel is based on a brief incident in the *Shui hu chuan* (nos. **99, 100**). The wealthy, unscrupulous merchant Hsi-men, after committing adultery with Golden Lotus (Chin-lien) who murders her husband, adds her to his household consisting already of a wife and three concubines. Other women enter the household, but the novel focuses on the relationship between Hsi-men and Golden Lotus, a ruthless, self-centered nymphomaniac who eventually causes Hsi-men's debilitation through sexual excesses. The last third of the novel concerns the members of Hsi-men's household after his death.

Chin P'ing Mei is not only the first novel of social criticism, it is also the first holistic one; while previous novels were characterized by episodic arrangements, the *Chin P'ing Mei*, although continuing many of the traditions of the storytellers such as the inclusion of song sequences, is the product of one man's imagination. Each episode is constructed to illustrate the character of the protagonist, one of his wives, or the social ills of the time. Furthermore, there is a new emphasis on characterization, especially of women. The characters in the novel are recognizably human, rather than heroes of epic proportions as in the earlier novels.

The late Ming period saw a large production of eroticism in literature and the visual arts, but this is only one explanation for its existence in the novel. While the explicit sexual scenes are perhaps unnecessary in the early part of the *Chin P'ing Mei*, they are crucial to the later parts. For it is the abnormal sexual drive and excessive behavior of Golden Lotus that leads to the downfall and death of the protagonist. Readers will find in C. T. Hsia's excellent discussion of the *Chin P'ing Mei* (see no. **95**, pp. 194–195 and 199), translations of brief erotic passages that are essential to the story. The first depicts Golden Lotus's increased control over Hsi-men; the second, the results of the sexual excesses that cause Hsi-men's physical collapse. In each case, the erotic passages are far from pornographic; indeed they lead to feelings of revulsion.

The infamous erotic portions of the novel are unfortunately not available to the English reader. The nearly complete translation by Clement Egerton, who was aided by the novelist Lao She (nos. **137, 138**), is in general accurate and readable. However, following the Victorian practice, the erotic passages are in Latin. This version includes a very brief, inadequate introduction and a list of the principal characters. The version by Franz Kuhn is abridged and all of the erotic passages were expurgated. Neither Franz Kuhn nor Bernard Miall, the translator into English, is given acknowledgment in the United States edition. There is a short but excellent footnoted introduction by Arthur Waley, and it is Waley's name only that is listed on the title page.

The *Ko-lien hua-ying* (Flower Shadows Behind the Curtain), by an unknown author, written in the middle of the seventeenth century, is a deliberate continuation of the *Chin P'ing Mei*. The plot centers on Hsi-men's first wife, Moon Lady, and her son during the twelfth century when Northern China was overrun by barbarians. The English edition includes an introduction on the history of the text by Franz Kuhn and a list of the principal characters.

110. Li Yü. *Jou Pu Tuan (The Prayer Mat of Flesh)*. Tr. by Richard Martin from the German version by Franz Kuhn. New York: Grove Press, 1963. 376 pp. (Paperback).

The *Jou p'u t'uan* (Prayer Mat of Flesh) is an erotic novel of the first half of the seventeenth century traditionally but controversially ascribed to Li Yü (1611–1680), a major literary figure of his day. The introductory chapter (placed at the end of the work in the Kuhn version) begins with the verse: "Listen and give ear. We are living in a day of unrestrained license. It is time to call a halt. The narration of erotic episodes is not an end in itself. It serves to gain a hearing for the voice of reason." The essay following this verse praises a moderate sexual life limited to one's wife (or wives) and states that the purpose of the novel is to teach, in a fashion designed to hold the reader's interest, the disastrous consequence of the unchaste life. Whether the novel is actually didactic or merely a work of pornography with a moralistic veneer remains a controversy. The sexual escapades in the story are not only explicit but often ludicrous as well; the humor serves to maintain interest despite a plethora of erotic scenes.

The plot is simple. A handsome, intelligent, but sensual young literatus visits a famous Buddhist hermit monk who recognizes him as his future disciple and urges him to take up the religious life immediately. The young scholar, not taking the hermit seriously, says that he is not ready and first must win the most beautiful woman in the world. Soon after leaving the hermit, he marries the daughter of a rigid puritanical Confucian scholar. He educates her, changing her frigidity to passion and then, bored, leaves her for other adventures. He meets a master burglar and the two declare themselves brothers, the burglar to aid in the young hero's seductions. But first discovering his natural "equipage" too small for the proposed tasks, the young scholar undergoes an absurd operation to increase its size to majestic proportions and then enters upon a series of sexual escapades. Meanwhile, the husband of a woman involved in the first of these escapades decides to revenge himself via the protagonist's own wife. He debauches her, leads her to run away from home, and sells her to a brothel, where she becomes a famous courtesan. Disgusted with himself, the revenged husband finds his way to the hermit mentioned in the beginning of the novel and enters the religious life. Eventually the young literatus seeks out the famous courtesan. Upon recognizing her client as her husband, she hangs herself; and he, realizing the truth of the prophecy of the hermit, becomes his disciple and is later joined by the master burglar.

It is the inventive composition and tight construction rather than the story that mark the *Jou p'u t'uan* as a superior literary work. Because of its fine craftsmanship and obvious original authorship, it is quite different from the novels which preceded it. The *Jou p'u t'uan* is also historically important, for although the late Ming dynasty saw the production of many erotic works of art both in literature and the graphic arts, in the more puritanical Ch'ing dynasty these works became extremely scarce and many were lost. Unfortunately, the often inaccurate Kuhn version, which has no introductory material, precludes a suitable understanding of the novel for many readers. The translator's note by Franz Kuhn at the end of the work, although informative, is lacking in accuracy.

111. Ts'ao Chan [Ts'ao Hsüeh-ch'in]. *The Dream of the Red Chamber.* Tr. by Florence and Isabel McHugh from the German version of Franz Kuhn. New York: Pantheon Books, 1958. xxi, 582 pp. (Paperback, Grosset & Dunlap).

112. ———. *Dream of the Red Chamber.* Tr. by Wang Chi-chen with a preface by Mark Van Doren. New York: Twayne Publishers, 1958. xxiv, 574 pp. (Abridged paperback, Anchor Books).

113. Rexroth, Kenneth. "Classics Revisited—XXI." *Saturday Review* 49 (Jan. 1, 1966): 19.

114. Hsia, C. T. "Love and Compassion in the *Dream of the Red Chamber.*" *Criticism* 5 (1963): 261–71.

The *Hung lou meng* (Dream of the Red Chamber) is undoubtedly China's greatest novel and is accorded an honored place among the world's literary masterpieces by a number of Western critics. Within the corpus of Chinese fiction, the *Dream* is unusual in a number of respects: it is semiautobiographical, possesses a profound literary maturity, demonstrates a rich and subtle imagination, and most important, reveals penetrating psychological insight. Following the literary revolution of the early twentieth century, Chinese scholars became so interested in this novel that a separate field of study, *hung-hsüeh* ("Red Studies"), developed.

The author, Ts'ao Chan (d. 1763), grew up at a time when his family's power and wealth were rapidly declining. The hero of the novel, Chia Pao-yü (Precious Jade), grows up in a parallel situation. Because Pao-yü has a sensitive, artistic temperament and a precocious interest in female society, he is often in trouble with his stern and proper Confucian father. There is tragedy in the frustrated love between Pao-yü and his cousin Lin Tai-yü (Black Jade). Orphaned in childhood, she was raised by their grandmother, a typical aristocratic old woman who indulges the whims of her favorite grandchildren. When Pao-yü is forced to marry another cousin, Lin T'ai-yü, who has always been frail, dies of a broken heart.

This romantic plot is only one of many strands within the novel. There is the tragic conflict between artistic temperament and the world of convention. Framing the whole novel is the world of Taoist legend and metaphysics. A magical sentient stone, imbued with the experience of the Universe, is transformed into a small piece of jade found in the mouth of Pao-yü at his birth. The stone is also linked to the birth of the heroine, Lin Tai-yü. The world of Buddhist and Taoist renunciation conflicts with the luxurious atmosphere of the family mansion. At the end of the novel, Pao-yü becomes a Buddhist monk. (The authorship of the last third of the novel is controversial).

The English rendering of Kuhn's incomplete German translation considerably reduces the esthetic quality of the novel with its awkward, simplistic language. Nevertheless, it is preferable to the more popular abridged translation of Wang Chi-chen which, because of its emphasis on Chinese customs and the picturesque, departs far from the tone and mood of the original, subverting it into a novel of manners.

As an aid to understanding the novel, two supplementary works are recommended. The first is the review essay by Kenneth Rexroth, which offers the general reader a brief but sympathetic and penetrating summary and analysis. Rexroth aptly expresses the impact of a Chinese novel upon the Western reader.

When you first read about all these people with strange names doing curious things in an exotic setting, you get lost. Then gradually the sheer human mass of Chinese fiction, a mass whose components are all highly individualistic, envelops and entrances you. You realize yourself as part of a universe of human beings endless as the dust of nebulae visible in the Mount Palomar telescope, and you are left with the significance of a human kinship powerful as flowing water and standing-stone.

Rexroth interestingly views *Hung lou meng* as a mystical Taoist work, the hero as "a Taoist saint who doesn't know he is one and doesn't want to be one."

The best article available in which the novel is examined in depth from a purely literary point of view is the supplementary piece by C. T. Hsia. Hsia considers the opposition of compassion and detachment within the author, his clinging to love as both *eros* and *agape* in conflict with his intellectual preference for Taoist renunciation, to be the tragic substance of the novel.

115. Wu Ching-tzu. *The Scholars.* Tr. by Yang Hsien-yi and Gladys Yang. Peking: Foreign Languages Press, 1957. 721 pp.

116. Kral, Oldrich. "Several Artistic Methods in the Classic Chinese Novel *Ju-lin Wai-shih." Archiv Orientalni* 32 (1964): 16–43.

Wu Ching-tzu (1701–54), precocious as a youth, was unsuccessful in the higher civil service examinations and refused or was unable to sit for a special examination. Although he had some fame as an author and had inherited an independent income, because of financial incompetency he spent his later life in relative poverty. He wrote a novel based partly on incidents from his own and his friends' and acquaintances' lives entitled *Ju-lin wai-shih* (lit., "Unofficial History of the Forest of Scholars") that satirized official life and the world of the literati.

The novel is in episodic form, often with little unity between the chapters. The first and last chapter concern paragons of Confucian virtue ignored by the high officials, while the remainder satirizes not only the worst elements of the Chinese civil service system, but of the whole Chinese social order as well. *The Scholars* is written exclusively from the Confucian viewpoint, in contrast to previous novels (for example, the *Chin P'ing Mei* incorporates the popular Buddhist view of retribution). The moralizing is indirect; the stories make their point without additional didactic commentary.

Aside from the manner in which satire and moralizing is applied in the novel, there are a number of other innovations. There are autobiographical elements, sparse use of the usual storyteller's conventions, consistent use of the vernacular, emphasis on realism, and new methods of characterization. Oldrich Kral points out in his interesting article on the methods of characterization utilized in *The Scholars:* "In his novel Wu Ching-tzu pursued the aim of presenting a broad and generalizing picture of a whole social stratum through the medium of a number of clearly cut vivid characters."

The complete literal English translation by Yang and Yang, while lacking in grace, preserves the tone and mood of the original. Included in the Foreign Languages Press edition are a helpful list of the principal characters, an appendix describing the examination system and the official ranks mentioned in the novel, a number of plates by Cheng Shih-fa illustrating the stories, and an extensive foreword by Wu Tsu-hsiang, Professor of Chinese Literature at Peking University. The latter provides an excellent introduction to the novel, despite the ideological position voiced by the writer.

117. van Gulik, Robert. *The Chinese Bell Murders.* New York: Harper and Brothers, 1958. 221 pp. (Paperback).

118. ———. *The Chinese Lake Murders*. New York: Harper and Brothers, 1960. 211 pp. (Paperback).

119. ———. *The Chinese Mail Murders*. New York: Harper and Row, 1961. 231 pp. (Paperback).

120. *T'ang-yin pi-shih*. *T'ang-yin pi-shih: Parallel Cases from under the Peartrees: A Thirteenth Century Manual of Jurisprudence and Detection*. Sinica Leidensia Series, vol. 10. Leiden: E. J. Brill, 1956. xiv, 198 pp.

Although these detective novels by the late Robert van Gulik (1910–1967), one of the foremost and most versatile sinologists and a noted diplomat in the Netherlands foreign service, are not usually considered Chinese literature, they were published in Chinese and Japanese before their English editions. And because they were with but few changes written in the style of the traditional Chinese novel, they are placed in this section rather than the one on twentieth-century literature. In their English versions, the novels received critical acclaim as superior detective stories.

Each novel is based on three detective stories of the type previously discussed (nos. **93**, **94**) woven into a single continuous story of short novel length, centering on "Judge Dee." There are a number of novels in the series which, if bound together, would form one full-length episodic novel tracing Judge Dee's early career. Unfortunately, the English versions have been variously published in a number of different countries and few libraries in the United States possess all of them. Judge Dee (Ti Jen-chieh, ca. 630–700) was historically an important statesman of the T'ang dynasty. In his early career as a magistrate in the outlying provinces, he gained fame for the many difficult criminal cases he solved. Because of this reputation, he became the hero of many later crime stories which had little historical basis.

The novels are written in the style of the Ming novels and set in the Ming period. The novelistic conventions maintained include the chapter titles summarizing the contents, the chapter introductory verse, the writing style, the introductory chapter involving the supernatural, the final summary chapter, and the description of the execution of the criminals and the reward of the magistrate. The differences lie in his limiting of the characters in the novel to a number manageable to Western and modern East Asian readers and in the recording of the crime as the magistrate solves it, rather than at the beginning as in the traditional stories. Van Gulik's thorough knowledge of Chinese life, customs and institutions of the Ming period is apparent in the well-presented wealth of background detail. These light novels provide the reader with not only enjoyment but possibly the best general introduction to traditional Chinese civilization.

Readers of the stories are encouraged to read the informative postscripts in the above-listed editions, where the author presents background material on Chinese jurisprudence and customs relevant to the plot. Those who become interested in this subject may wish to read van Gulik's scholarly translation of a thirteenth-century casebook, the *T'ang-yin pi-shih* (Parallel Cases from under the Pear Tree).

Twentieth-Century Literature

121. Hsia, C. T. *A History of Modern Chinese Fiction.* 2d ed. New Haven: Yale University Press, 1971. xiii, 701 pp. (Paperback).

This first major survey of modern Chinese fiction as well as the first serious study utilizing the techniques of contemporary American and English literary criticism is intended for the general reader: "I covet readers who know little about modern China but are curious about its literature." Divided into three chronological parts (1917–27, 1928–37, and 1937–57), the study emphasizes individual authors; twelve of the nineteen chapters discuss the writings of eleven of the most important. Available in these discussions are plot summaries and translated passages from major works.

To Professor Hsia, the most brilliant literary period was the 1930s; the decline was primarily due to Communist obscurantism. Of the better modern Chinese fiction, "its first characteristic is its sober examination of contemporary life in China. This realism is accompanied by a sense of pity, considerable satire, and some serious attempt toward an imaginative understanding of Chinese society as a whole."

In the first edition, Tsi-an Hsia, then the editor of the Taiwan publication *Literary Review,* supplied a short, perceptive, and informed appendix on the literary situation in Taiwan. Because leftist Chinese literature in the main is rigidly proscribed by the Kuomintang government, Tsi-an Hsia finds "the most distressing literary phenomenon about Taiwan is its refusal to take cognizance of the immediate past"; the youth are cut off from the literature of the past generation. Most fiction written in Taiwan, aside from the usually trite anti-Communist propaganda, is of the escapist romantic variety. C. T. Hsia dropped this essay from his second edition because he notes the high quality of some recent anti-Communist fiction. However, as he points out, these novels have not been well received in Taiwan and the authors are still living a precarious existance.

The second edition contains an epilogue, "Communist Literature Since 1958," the year the antirightist campaign was concluded. In this section, the author discusses several novels (available in translation) written in the late fifties and one work of the mid-sixties sponsored by the People's Liberation Army. Professor Hsia discourses on the continuing deterioration of Chinese fiction from a literary standpoint, but his strong criticism of contemporary Chinese Communism and its suppression of Western-influenced fiction is untempered by an explanation of what the Chinese are attempting to do with their civilization, society, and culture.

In the second edition, his brother's essay is replaced by two appendices. In "Obsession With China: The Moral Burden of Modern Chinese Literature," Professor Hsia discusses satirical novels, including Lao She's *Cat Country (no.* **138)**, and *The Whirlwind,* a novel written in Taiwan in the fifties. The volume concludes with an extensive glossary and bibliography.

122. Scott, A. C. *Literature and the Arts in Twentieth Century China.* (1963). Gloucester, Massachusetts: Peter Smith, 1968. xix, 212 pp.

Two of the eight chapters are concerned with literature: "Literature" (pp. 9–34) and "The Chinese Outside China" (pp. 153–188). Within these few pages (only twenty excluding poetry in the chapter on literature), Professor Scott presents a capable, compact introduction to the subject. The "Literature" chapter includes a historical introduction, a discussion of the major writers, and a brief analysis of "the war period" and "the contemporary scene." "The Chinese outside China" looks at the literary developments of the Chinese in Hong Kong, Taiwan, England, and the United States: Lin Yutang of the United States, for example, is discussed here. The volume provides a list of the personalities discussed, a select bibliography, and an index.

Of interest is Professor Scott's chapter on the cinema. The most proficient Chinese film company today is Shaw Brothers of Hong Kong and Singapore, where Professor Scott observes an unfortunate tendency to produce films of popular rather than artistic appeal. However, discernible in these technically superb, popular productions, is an interesting extension of traditional literature into a new popular form. The tales told by the Sung storytellers, which became dramas in the Yüan period and novels in the early Ming dynasty, are now conveyed through the modern medium of film. These stories, often adopting Ming costume and customs, with specially written music that combines both the Ming and modern Western idiom, indicate that these traditional tales will ever remain popular among the Chinese.

123. Ting Yi. *A Short History of Modern Chinese Literature*. Peking: Foreign Languages Press, 1959. 310 pp.

A companion volume in the "China Knowledge Series" to Feng Yüan-chün's *A Short History of Classical Chinese Literature* (no. **13**), this work consists of the lecture notes of Ting Yi, who died in 1954 before he finished his revisions. The book begins with the May Fourth Movement of 1919 and follows the historical trend in literature to the Congress of Writers and Artists of 1949.

Because this work is thoroughly imbued with the Chinese Communist view of literature and deals exclusively with the modern period, it is of limited value to the general Western reader. However, if the reader understands the ideological principles on which Ting's lectures are based, he will find that this compact discussion of the modern Chinese view of the evolution of their own literature merits attention. The focus is on the development of orthodoxy, and one underlying assumption is that there is a correct attitude toward literature; hence, the reader encounters discussions about wrong views.

No translations from the literary works themselves are provided in the discussions, though there are numerous excerpts from various statements of authors on the growth of their own personal ideological views. The English translations—the various chapters were rendered into English by six different translators—are uneven and awkward, but the intent is usually clear. An index with the Chinese characters is provided.

124. Li Tien-yi. "Continuity and Change in Modern Chinese Literature." *Annals of the American Academy of Political and Social Sciences* 321 (January 1959): 90–99.

The title of this excellent brief article describes its contents. Professor Li discusses the changes in Chinese literature since the Literary Revolution of 1917: the replacement of the classical language with the vernacular, the emphasis on realism with subsequent interest in "revolutionary literature," and the growth of left-wing influence. The Chinese Communist approach to literature is examined, especially the policy of "Socialist Realism" since 1949. The concept of "realism," shown to have historical antecedents, is emphasized as one aspect of continuity in Chinese literary history.

125. Chow Tse-tsung. *The May Fourth Movement: Intellectual Revolution in Modern China.* Harvard East Asian Studies, 6. Cambridge: Harvard University Press, 1960. 486 pp. (Paperback, Stanford University Press).

The student demonstration in Peking on May 4, 1919, reflecting the intense disappointment with the Versailles Peace Conference and marking the fourth anniversary of the still-felt indignation and humiliation of Japan's Twenty-one Demands, is generally considered the pivotal point in the development of contemporary Chinese history. The movement that arose from this demonstration, "The May Fourth Movement," had widespread effects, including the reorganization of the Kuomintang and the birth of the Chinese Communist Party. Chow Tse-tsung, in his superb scholarly study of this movement, thoroughly covers its development from 1915 to 1923 and provides a detailed analysis of the main intellectual currents.

One of the most important effects of the May Fourth Movement was the rapid advancement of the literary revolution. The establishment of a new vernacular literature greatly facilitated popular education and "exerted far-reaching influences upon the intellectual trends of China in later decades." Chapter eleven (pp. 269–288), "The Literary Revolution," which covers the development of twentieth-century prose writing, is especially recommended. Here Professor Chow discusses the old literature, the advocacy of realism, the vernacular in literary writing and opposition to its use, and the development of revolutionary literature.

126. Yuan Chia-hua, and Payne, Robert, eds. and trs. *Contemporary Chinese Short Stories*. London & New York: Noel Carrington, 1946. 169 pp.

This work is an excellent collection of eleven of the best short stories written in China from the 1920s through the early forties. The nine authors represented, including such well-known writers as Lu Hsün, Lao She, Yang Chen-sheng, Shih Che-ts'un and Chang T'ien-i, were all born, except for Lu Hsün, between 1891 and 1908, and hence write about a similar period in recent Chinese history from a number of individual perspectives.

Half of the stories involve the military, three concerning themselves directly with the guerilla activities against the Japanese. But these stories, rather than reflecting the larger issues, show the participants as human beings concerned with their immediate lives and situations. Most of the stories, especially those of Tuan-mu Hung-liang, illustrate the poverty of the peasants and the rapaciousness of the landlords. Some—for example Yang Chen-sheng's "The Anchor," the story of the murder of a bully in a peasant fishing village by a drunken mob—are universal in nature. The earliest story, "The Waves of the Wind" by Lu Hsün, deals with the period immediately following the revolution and the restoration of the Boy Emperor P'u Yi to the throne for eighty-seven days in 1917. A man who had his pigtail (the symbol of Manchu occupation) cut off after the overthrow of the Ch'ing dynasty fears for his life when it seems that the old customs might be forcibly restored.

Many of these stories have more or less been influenced by European literature, but the pervading presence of compassion, even in the face of violence, of humanness, even in crowded conditions and abject poverty, is perhaps uniquely Chinese. The translations into English are among the best that have been done in this genre of literature. They read with a vividness and immediacy that do justice to the originals. An excellent short introduction to modern Chinese literature is provided.

127. Snow, Edgar, ed. and comp. *Living China: Modern Chinese Short Stories*. New York: John Day Co., n.d. (Introduction

dated 1936). New York: Reynal & Hitchcock, 1937. 360 pp.

128. Wang Chi-chen, tr. *Contemporary Chinese Stories.* (1944). Connecticut: Greenwood Press, 1969.

129. Milton, Daniel L. and Clifford, William, eds. *A Treasury of Modern Asian Stories.* Paperbound. New York: The New American Library, Mentor Books, 1961. 237 pp.

Edgar Snow, a well-known journalist who had unusually close relations with many important Chinese leaders, intellectuals, and writers in the 1930s, compiled an anthology of contemporary short stories that is striking in the feeling of immediacy it imparts. With the exception of the story by Lin Yutang, which was written originally in English, the stories were translated in conjunction with the authors or with other Chinese writers and were interpreted rather than translated literally. While this practice is normally to be condemned, here it has been quite successful. In his interesting introduction, Edgar Snow explains the reasons for the various changes from the Chinese originals.

The volume is divided into two parts, the first consisting of seven stories by Lu Hsün, preceded by his biography. The second part includes seventeen short stories by the fourteen most important vernacular short story writers of the 1920s and 1930s. Each story is preceded by a short, compact introduction. Because many authors were at least as interested in alleviating the social ills of China as in composing literature, these stories present a view of warlordism, poverty, and changing social mores in late nineteenth- and early twentiety-century China, a view that is otherwise difficult to obtain.

One finds in this anthology too, stories about the conflict between the Communist movement and the Nationalist government. An appendix, "The Modern Chinese Literary Movement," by Nym Wales, is a very good leftist introduction to the subject, emphasizing the struggles between the various factions, and the suppressions and executions of the leftist writers by the Nationalists (Kuomintang). An annotated bibliography is also included.

The anthology by Wang Chi-chen lacks an introduction and suffers from the same translation difficulties found in his companion volume, *Traditional Chinese Tales* (no. **80**). There are notes on the authors at the end. The selection of twenty-one stories by twelve authors is good, and does not duplicate any of the stories in *Living China*. A glossary of Chinese words and honorifics is provided to cover both *Contemporary Chinese Stories* and *Traditional Chinese Stories*, but many of the terms could have been more conveniently translated within the text. For example, *didi* ("younger brother") is frequently used in one story where "my brother" would have been clearer to the Western reader, especially when it was established by the translator in the first sentence that the subject is the narrator's younger brother.

A Treasury of Modern Asian Stories is an inexpensive paperback with an excellent selection of twentieth-century stories from most Asian languages. The seven Chinese stories (pp. 166–213) were taken from Edgar Snow and Wang Chi-chen's abovementioned works. They provide a representative assortment of modern short stories, each by an outstanding Chinese author.

130. Liu E. [Liu T'ieh-yün] *The Travels of Lao Ts'an.* Tr. and annot. by Harold Shadick (1952). Ithaca: Cornell University Press, 1966. xxiii, 277 pp. (Paperback).

131. Lin Yutang, tr. *A Nun of T'aishan and Other Translations.* Shanghai: Commercial Press, 1936. 276 pp.

132. ———. *Widow, Nun and Courtesan: Three Novelettes from the Chinese.* (1951). Connecticut: Greenwood Press, 1971. vi, 266 pp.

Liu E (Liu T'ieh-yün, 1857–1909) was one of the most important southern novelists of the early twentieth century who dealt with social satire of the type originated in the *Ju-lin wai-shih* (no. **115**). He was well educated, but refused to study the stilted and otherwise useless essay form required in the official examinations. In his youth he was part of a group that was preparing for the crisis they felt was certain to come to China. Liu E studied flood control, music, astronomy, and medicine. He became a disciple of a syncretistic religious society that combined elements of Confucianism, Buddhism, and Taoism. Unsuccessful as a practitioner of traditional Chinese medicine, he started a printing establishment in Shanghai, one of the first to use the lithographic process, but became involved in a lawsuit and went bankrupt.

In 1888, following a major flood of the Yellow River, Liu E was given a responsible position repairing the dikes and was quite successful. He was then invited by a governor to be an advisor on flood control and there rose to the rank of prefect. Disputes concerning flood control methods earned him the enmity of important officials which later cost him his life. After a period of mourning for his mother in 1891, he spent two years in the Foreign Office in Peking where he became convinced that commerce and industry were essential for China to become strong and that these were dependent on railroads. He promoted the building of railroads, which roused the anatagonism of others. Liu E finally gave up his government career and attempted a number of commercial and industrial projects, all of which failed.

After the Boxer Rebellion, because of his friendship with foreign diplomats, Liu was involved in negotiating the treaty that ended the foreign occupations. Again he attempted a number of unsuccessful business ventures. In 1904, he started writing *Lao-ts'an yu-chi* (The Travels of Lao Ts'an) to help a friend out financially. The chapters were printed in various magazines and newspapers while he continued to start unsuccessful businesses. In 1908 his enemies, among whom was Yüan Shih-k'ai, succeeded in having him banished and Liu E died during the arduous journey.

The Travels of Lao Ts'an, the only writing of this sort attempted by the author, is of the episodic type. As it was written and published chapter by chapter, in parts it lacks a sense of unity. The novel reflects many of the events and influences of the author's life. Lao Ts'an is an educated man who refuses official life and lives as an itinerant practitioner of Chinese medicine, at which he is quite successful. An archetypal Taoist sage, he advises officials who seek his assistance but refuses all honors. The novel traces several adventures he and his friends encounter, including the solution of difficult criminal cases and a long episode in a mountain abode of immortals. The novel is especially notable for its descriptive passages, which provide a heightened sense of realism.

Throughout the novel, Liu E expresses himself on a number of different subjects, especially in the realm of moral and political philosophy. Although he was opposed to violent revolution, one reason for the novel's popularity was that it was accepted as a prophetic work—it forecast a revolution in 1910, only one year off the mark.

Although thirty-four chapters were published in the *Tientsin Daily News*, most editions consist of only twenty chapters, as does the masterful translation by Harold Shadick, which is both close to the original Chinese and eminently readable. The edition includes an extensive introduction, thorough notes at the end of the volume, an appendix elucidating the poems in the novel, a glossary, and a map and key to pronunciation. All in all, this is the finest English version of a Chinese novel available.

Chapters twenty through twenty-six have been translated by Lin Yutang with the title *A Nun of T'aishan*, published in 1936. This volume also contains translations of seven modern humorous stories and two groups of miscellany under the title "Ancient Chinese Humor" and "Classical Sketches." Lin Yutang later published an improved translation of these six chapters in *Widow, Nun and Courtesan*, adding to it the tale, "Widow Chuan" by Lao Hsiang (Wang Hsiang-ch'en), and an original story by Lin Yutang entitled "Miss Tu."

133. Lu Hsün [Chou Shu-jen]. *Ah Q and Others: Selected Stories of Lusin*. Tr. by Wang Chi-chen. (1941). Connecticut: Greenwood Press, 1971. xxvii, 219 pp.

134. ———. *Selected Works of Lu Hsün*. Tr. by Yang Hsien-yi and Gladys Yang. 4 vols. Peking: Foreign Languages Press. 1956–1960. 440, 364, 343, and 312 pp.

Lu Hsün (Chou Shu-jen, 1881–1936) is the most popular and the most famous modern Chinese author. Following his death, the Communist Party raised him to the status of a cultural saint. As a youth, he received a government scholarship and went to Japan, where he studied medicine. There he was influenced by Western writings, especially those of Nietzsche, Darwin, and the Russian authors. Lu Hsün dropped his study of medicine, feeling he could best serve China as a writer. At first, writing in the literary language, he was unsuccessful. But after the Literary Revolution in 1917, he began to write in the spoken language and rapidly rose to prominence.

Lu Hsün primarily wrote short stories and essays, often of a satirical nature, attacking tradition-bound, backward, ethnocentric attitudes. Lu Hsün felt that for China to survive, she must break with her past and terminate the political chaos, and it was to these ends that he directed his efforts.

Ah Q and Others contains eleven of Lu Hsün's best-known stories and an extensive introduction by Wang Chi-chen. "The Diary of a Madman," published in 1918, the last story in the collection, was the first story he wrote after the Literary Revolution. This story, like his others, is symbolic. (The title was taken from Gogol but is otherwise unrelated.) It consists of random jottings from the diary of a man who is temporarily insane. Under the delusion of paranoia, he comes to believe that his relatives and friends are planning to eat him and alludes to various historical incidents and writings to prove that cannibalism has existed in China. Cannibalism symbolizes Chinese traditional morality: each person surviving by "eating" others. The story ends with the cry, "maybe there are still some infants that have not yet eaten men. Save, save the infants . . ." In the prologue to the story, the madman has recovered his sanity and is awaiting an official appointment; recovered, he is back in the midst of the old morality.

"The True Story of Ah Q" is Lu Hsün's best-known story. Ah Q (written in Chinese with the Western "Q" because the author pretends not to know which character is meant by his name "K'uei") represents the worst aspects of Chinese society of Lu Hsün's time, and the story is an acute analysis of more recent Chinese history. Although the village bum, Ah Q constantly deludes himself about his superior character. He has an ingrained defeatist attitude, but readily browbeats those weaker than himself. Always losing in his mean confrontation with others, he is quick to find moral victory in his defeat:

Ah Q inevitably lost and ended up by being held by the queue while his head was thumped noisily against the wall. This was of course only an outward defeat. After his adversary had gone with the laurels of victory, Ah Q would say to himself, 'I have been beaten by my son. What a world we live in today!' and he too would go off satisfied and spiritually victorious. [p. 84].

Ah Q dreams he is one of the revolutionaries, but when the revolutionaries do arrive, they join forces with the local gentry and execute Ah Q for a robbery he did not commit.

The first volume of the *Selected Works of Lu Hsün* contains Lu Hsün's short stories, prose poems, and reminiscences. Of the eleven stories in the Wang edition, ten can also be found here. Volumes two through four contain Lu Hsün's essays and random notes arranged chronologically. *A Brief History of Chinese Fiction* (see no. **15**), is an excellent example of Lu Hsün's scholarly writings.

135. Mao Tun [Shen Yen-ping]. *Midnight.* (No. translator listed). Peking: Foreign Languages Press, 1957. 524 pp.

136. ————. *Spring Silkworms and Other Stories.* Tr. by Sidney Shapiro. Peking: Foreign Languages Press, 1956. 278 pp.

Mao Tun (Shen Yen-ping, b. 1896) is one of the best twentieth-century Chinese authors and has been an important figure in Chinese letters since the 1920s. Following the founding of the People's Republic in 1949, he was named Minister of Culture and vice-chairman of the federation of writers and artists. Previously he had been a teacher and newspaper editor as well as a popular prose and fiction writer.

Tzu yeh (Midnight), written in 1933, is a treatment of the complex Chinese industrial situation in 1930. The English version includes an excerpt from a talk by the author on how and why he came to write the novel. Although Mao Tun had planned to cover problems in both the city and the country, he was only able to deal with the former. Demonstrating considerable research, Mao Tun sought to prove that China "was being reduced to the status of a colony under the pressure of imperialism." The hero of the novel, Wu Sun-fu, is a powerful Shanghai industrialist who strives to save China by industrializing the country with native capital. Doomed to failure by the then current situation, his efforts only leave him bankrupt. Woven around this theme are numerous subplots, including the rise of Communism. The Western reader, unfamiliar with the concerns and struggles of that period, may find the novel somewhat tedious. This difficulty should not be encountered in Mao Tun's short stories.

Spring Silkworms and Other Stories is a collection of thirteen well-translated stories by Mao Tun, all but one written between 1930 and 1936. The volume includes a politically slanted editor's note and a biography of the author.

"Spring Silkworms," "Autumn Harvest," and "Winter Ruin" form a trilogy that traces the destruction of a once financially comfortable family. "Spring Silkworms" is considered by C. T. Hsia to be "Mao Tun's best story and perhaps the outstanding achievement in Chinese proletarian fiction" (no. 121). In this story, the family has already lost their fortune: inequitable foreign trade has drastically lowered the price of raw silk while raising the price of the things the family must buy. Spring promises a bumper crop of silkworms (there is a fascinating account of raising silkworms), and the family sinks everything it has left into the purchase of mulberry leaves. Their hope is fulfilled, but there is no market. And so, the family finds itself like the rest of the village ruinously in debt even after an unusually successful crop—there is no way out and no hope.

This theme is repeated in "Autumn Harvest." The starving villagers raid the town merchants for rice, but the elder of the family of the previous story condemns them. He holds to the traditional view of righteousness, that only through honest labor can they feed themselves and get out of debt. His sons do not even wish to plant rice, believing that it will only sink them deeper into debt. But the rice is planted, money is borrowed for fertilizer and for water during a severe drought, the crop is saved—and the rice merchants drastically lower the price! Again after bitter hard labor, they are further in debt; the old man gives up his moral beliefs as well as his life.

In "Winter Ruin," the villagers are desperate and come to believe that a new dynasty will soon begin, bringing order again to their world. The local security force of three, hired with the peasants' money by the wealthy to protect them from the peasants, capture a young boy and beat him because he is believed to be the new young emperor destined to rise and save China. The villagers, led by the eldest son of the family whose story is being told, rescue him and kill the soldiers. The boy is sent home, but now with three rifles in the villagers' hands, one senses the beginning of a real revolution.

137. Lao She [Shu Ch'ing-ch'un]. *Rickshaw Boy*. Tr. by Evan King. New York: Reynal & Hitchcock, 1945; Garden City: Sun Dial, 1946. 315 pp.

138. ———. *Cat Country*. Tr. by William A. Lyell, Jr. Columbus: Ohio State University Press, 1970. xliii, 295 pp.

Lao She (Shu Ch'ing-ch'un, 1899–?1966), born in Peking of Manchu descent, is the only major twentieth-century writer from North China. He resided in England from 1925 to 1930 and was influenced by the English novelists, especially Dickens. Although he is one of the writers of the literary revolution, Lao She is different from the other important novelists of the thirties in his removal of literature from ideological polemics. His novels, which demonstrate superior craftsmanship, emphasize the human and humorous aspects of life and the dignity and worth of even the lowliest in the social order.

According to C. T. Hsia, *Camel Hsiang-tsu* (*Rickshaw Boy* is a descriptive title), written in 1938, "may be taken as the finest modern Chinese novel up to that time . . . essentially an impassioned and tightly constructed novel of realistic integrity. Its crisp and racy language catches the very accent and flavor of the Peking vernacular, its principal characters are all memorably human" (no. **121**). The novel traces the deterioration and near destruction of an innocent farm youth in Peking during the chaotic period before the Sino-Japanese war; the cause, the real villain, is the social order.

The taut plot is readily summarized. Happy Boy (the translator follows the unfortunate practice of translating rather than transliterating Chinese names), an unusually tall and strong farm youth, comes to the city and takes up rickshaw pulling. His sole goal in life is to possess his own rickshaw and, after three years of utmost scrimping from the slight profit of pulling a rented vehicle, he manages to purchase one. Six months later, he is conscripted by force into a ragtag army band and his rickshaw is confiscated. He manages to escape with a few camels (hence his nickname), but the amount he realizes from their sale is less than a third of the purchase price of a rickshaw—and of this slight sum he is soon cheated. Seduced by Tiger Girl, the uncouth, ugly, middle-aged daughter of the rickshaw rental stable owner who likes him for his naive honesty, he is forced into a marriage for which he has no desire by her false claim of pregnancy. Thrown out by his father-in-law, the couple exists on Tiger Girl's considerable savings, which, however, she soon fritters away. Before the money is completely gone, she allows Happy Boy to purchase a rickshaw. But now she really is pregnant, and when she later dies in childbirth, Happy Boy is forced to sell the rickshaw to pay the burial expenses. Still bent on possessing his own vehicle, Happy Boy is now considerably reduced in spirit, morality, and health; indeed, he has even fallen beneath others of his class. Toward the close of the novel, he finds a kind professor for whom he had previously worked as a salaried rickshaw boy. The professor offers him back his job, and, in effect, his life, and is even willing to take in the girl he loves. This girl, Little Lucky One, had been forced to become a prostitute to support her brothers. At the very end of the novel, Happy Boy finds her dying in a low-class brothel and carries her off.

This weak ending was conceived by Evan King, the translator, not by Lao She. The total destruction of the protagonist rather than his being saved in the nick of time would have been more fitting to the novel as a whole. However, because of the excellent characterization and the tight, usually consistent intensity of the narrative, *Camel Hsiang-tzu* is recommended over all other modern Chinese novels to the Western reader.

An earlier work by Lao She, written in 1932, is a satirical novel written within a science-fiction framework (of the early thirties). The narrator is a member of a three-man crew on a Chinese spaceship to Mars. The ship crashes on arrival, his companions are killed, and he is captured by the local inhabitants, creatures that are very similar in appearance to cats. "Cat Country" is, of course, China from an alien perspective. Every aspect of Chinese civilization and society of the 1930s is satirized—acutely, effectively, and viciously: the role of women in society, the educational system, the military, the generation gap, home construction, public morality and especially the reaction of Chinese to foreigners in China, including the invading Japanese. Even with Lyell's helpful notes, knowledge of Chinese history of the last century and a half is needed to understand the satire; the novel is not advised for those who have only a cursory background on China. On the other hand, perhaps no other literary work available in translation from this period so well presents the case for the changes the Chinese have since brought about in their civilization—changes which are still taking place. One shudders to think what a Lao She today could do with American civilization.

To translate the idioms of one language into those of another is extremely difficult. The occasional noticeable failures in this excellent translation by Lyell, an authority on Chinese fiction of the early twentieth century, only serve to indicate how successful he has been. The translation is preceded by an introduction to the life and work of Lao She.

139. Pa Chin [Li Fei-kan]. *The Family.* Tr. by Sidney Shapiro. (1958). 2d. ed. Peking: Foreign languages Press, 1964. 322 pp. (Rev. paperback ed. with intro. by Olga Lang, Doubleday Anchor Books, 1972).

140. Lang, Olga. *Pa Chin and His Writings: Chinese Youth Between the Two Revolutions.* Harvard East Asian Series, 28. Cambridge: Harvard University Press, 1967. xiii, 402 pp.

Pa Chin (Li Fei-kan, b. 1904) has remained a popular author in China through the various political and ideological developments, but he is not one of the best modern writers. *Chia* (The Family), published in 1931, is the first part of the semiautobiographical trilogy, *Chi-liu* (Turbulent Stream), which depicts the decay of the Kao family during the turbulent years from 1919 to 1923. The heroes of *Turbulent Stream* are the youth of China successfully struggling against the old order in their efforts to modernize.

The Family primarily concerns three brothers. The eldest, Kao Chüeh-hsin, although sympathetic to his rebellious younger brothers, bows to the will of the family until the end of the novel. As a young man, he had been in love with his cousin, but acquiesced when his family wed him to another. (His cousin returns in the novel, a widow, to die of heartbreak and consumption). As the novel opens, Chüeh-hsin is happy with his wife and young son and is responsible for his orphaned brothers. At the end, his wife, forced out of her home by a superstitious custom to which he did not object, dies in childbirth.

The second brother, Chüeh-hui, the hero and the author's alter ego, is a strong-willed revolutionary, resisting the traditional way of life. The girl he loves, a bond-servant beneath his station, drowns herself when she is forced to be a concubine to an old man, a friend of the autocratic head of the household. Chüeh-hui encourages the youngest brother, Chüeh-min, in love with a cousin, to resist the family's plans for his marriage. The novel closes with Chüeh-hui, unable to endure life in the family compound any longer, fleeing to another city with his elder brother's help.

The villain in the novel is the traditional family/moral system; its destruction will resolve all difficulties. In Pa Chin's later, more mature works, the problems and solutions are no longer so simple or clear-cut. The argument in *The Family* is primarily emotional, on the level of a better soap opera. But if the Western reader does not encounter literary merit, he will find an apt description of life in a wealthy family in the midst of a civilization in revolution.

The Family was immensely popular and served as the basis for a play and two films. Its English translation is clean and easy to read, unencumbered by picturesque translations of names or excess verbiage. The occasional use of the British idiom within the Chinese context should not be disconcerting to American readers. A short biography of the author is included at the end of the volume. For a deeper insight into Pa Chin's life and writings, Olga Lang's scholarly study is recommended.

141. Chao Shu-li. *Changes in Li Village.* Tr. by Gladys Yang. Peking: Foreign Languages Press, 1953. 224 pp.

Chao Shu-li was, until his denunciation in 1967, considered one of the most important contemporary Chinese fiction writers by Communist critics. Not well educated (he only finished junior high school), he learned from his farmer-father the art of ballad-telling. Because of his peasant origins and unsophisticated upbringing, he was regarded as a people's author and his works have been quite popular.

The highly praised short novel, *Changes in Li Village,* first published in 1945, won a Stalin Second Prize in Literature in 1952. As the title states, the novel traces the trials and changes that take place in a northern Chinese village from the civil strife before the Japanese invasion to the end of the Second World War. The first half of the novel depicts with honest naiveté the downfall of a peasant, T'ieh-so, as he comes into conflict with the opium-smoking landlord-family controlling the corrupt village government. Stripped of most of his land and his home in an unjust court, T'ieh-so continually runs afoul of his tormentors, becoming at one point during the Japanese invasion, the personal servant and bodyguard of his chief tormentor. The landlord and his cronies, on the other hand, always seem to rise to the top—as army officers, Japanese collaborators, head of the pro-Communist village organization, and anti-Communist officials. In the process, they torture, kill and rob the peasants of the village, until the landlord is literally torn to shreds by the villagers at the end of the novel.

T'ieh-so eventually becomes a Communist organizer in his native village and an anti-Japanese guerilla. The second half of the novel is a simplistic, good-versus-evil story of the awakening of the peasants under the inspiration of the Communist cadres. The novel ends with the peasants preparing to defend their newly gained freedom against the return of the reactionary Kuomintang troops following the defeat of the Japanese (at the very time this was actually happening in Northern China). Hence as with all Communist literature, the novel is first, if not exclusively, a work of propaganda and will undoubtedly be found unsatisfactory as literature by most Western readers. The translation which would be improved by some obvious editing is published without introduction or notes.

142. Jenner, W. J. F., ed. *Modern Chinese Stories*. Tr. by W. J. F. Jenner and Gladys Yang. London: Oxford University Press, 1970. 271 pp. (Paperback).

The short stories, unfinished novelette, and tales from the 1920s to the mid-sixties contained in this volume were chosen, not for their literary merits, but to illustrate the attitudes of modern Chinese toward their problems and their means of overcoming these problems. The editor points this out in his brief but effective introduction: "In their formal and technical qualities the stories of nearly all modern Chinese writers except Lu Xun [Lu Hsün] have little to offer those in search of literary novelty and brilliance."

Stories included are by Lu Hsün, Mao Tun, Lao She and others, whose works, often superior ones, can be found in earlier collections. It is in its inclusion of material from the fifties and early sixties that this volume is important. Of interest are two modern storytellers' tales less than ten years old. Here we can see the continuation of the storyteller's art in its contemporary setting. The tales concern events based on heroes of the agricultural cooperatives during their formative years. Like the old tales, they contain a mixture of prose and song.

Most of the stories are concerned with rural China. One of the exceptions, and perhaps the best story from the post-World War II period, is "Maple Leaves," written by Ho Ku-yen in 1955, about the driver of a supply truck and his assistant during the Korean War. A very human and poignant story, it will serve to dispel the Western myth of Chinese callousness toward life; it will also help in understanding how the Vietnamese can continue to move supplies southward despite intensive U. S. aerial bombardment.

Aside from the general introduction, the individual stories are preceded by useful and interesting introductions, and the volume ends with a list of sources including the Chinese characters. The romanization used in this work is the Hanyu Pinyin adopted by the Communist government; it can be expected to become more common in future publications. The editor includes a brief note on pronunciation, but those familiar only with the Wade-Giles system, still standard in English-speaking countries, are liable to encounter difficulties.

FURTHER READINGS
UNANNOTATED

GENERAL WORKS:

Davidson, Martha. *A List of Published Translations from Chinese into English, French and German.* Part I: Literature Exclusive of Poetry. New Haven: Yale University Far Eastern Publications, 1952. 180 pp.

Hightower, James R. "Chinese Literature in the Context of World Literature." *Comparative Literature* 5 (1953): 117–124.

Li Tien-yi. *The History of Chinese Literature: A Selected Bibliography.* Sinological Series, 15. New Haven: Yale University Far Eastern Publications, 1968. 24 pp.

Prušek, Jaroslav. *Chinese History and Literature: Collection of Studies.* Dordrecht, Holland: D. Reidel Publishing Co., 1970. 587 pp. (distr. by Humanities Press, New York).

ANTHOLOGIES:

Kao, George [Kao K'o-i], ed. and tr. *Chinese Wit and Humor.* New York: Coward-McCann, 1946. xxxv, 347 pp.

CLASSICS:

The I-li or Book of Etiquette and Ceremonial. Tr. by John Steele. 2 vols. Probsthain's Oriental Series, vol. 8–9. London: Probsthain, 1917. 288 and 242 pp.

Li-chi. Tr. by James Legge. Vols. 27–28 in *Sacred Books of the East,* ed. by Max F. Müller. Oxford: Clarendon Press, 1885.

HISTORY:

Franke, Hans Hermann, *Catalogue of Translations From the Chinese Dynastic Histories for the Period 220–960.* Berkeley: University of California Press, 1957. 295 pp.

Gardiner, Charles S. *Traditional Chinese Historiography.* Harvard

Historical Monographs, no. 11. rev. ed. Cambridge: Harvard University Press, 1961. 121 pp.

PHILOSOPHY:

Chan Wing-tsit. *An Outline and Annotated Bibliography of Chinese Philosophy*. Frequently revised. New Haven: Yale University Far Eastern Publications, 1959.

Chu Hsi, and Lü Tsu-ch'ien, comps. *Reflections on Things at Hand: A Neo-Confucian Anthology*. Annot. and tr. by Chan Wing-tsit. New York: Columbia University Press, 1967. xli, 441 pp.

Creel, H. G. *"What is Taoism?" and Other Studies in Chinese Cultural History*. Chicago: University of Chicago Press, 1970. 192 pp.

Fung Yu-lan. *A History of Chinese Philosophy*. Tr. by Derk Bodde. 2 vols. Princeton: Princeton University Press, 1952–53. xxiv, 455 and xxv, 783 pp.

————. *A Short History of Chinese Philosophy*. Ed. and tr. by Derk Bodde. New York: Macmillan Co., 1948. xx, 368 pp. (Paperback).

————. *The Spirit of Chinese Philosophy*. Tr. by E. R. Hughes. London: Kegan Paul, 1947. xiv, 224 pp. (Paperback, Beacon Press).

Huai nan tzu. Tao the Great Luminant. Tr. by Evan Morgan. (1935). New York: Paragon Book Gallery, 1969. xlv, 291 pp.

Hughes, E. R. *Chinese Philosophy in Classical Times*. rev. ed. New York: E. P. Dutton & Co., Everyman's Library, 1954.

Wang Ch'ung. *Lun-heng*. Tr. by Alfred Forke. 2 vols. (1907). 2d ed. New York: Paragon Book Gallery, 1962. 577 and 536 pp.

Wang Yang-ming. *Instructions for Practical Living and Other Neo-Confucian Writings*. Annot. and tr. by Chan Wing-tsit. New York: Columbia University Press, 1963. 358 pp.

BELLES LETTRES:

Chinese Fables and Anecdotes. Peking: Foreign Languages Press, 1958. 52 pp.

Li Tien-yi. *Chinese Fiction: A Bibliography of Books and Articles in Chinese and English.* New Haven: Yale University Far Eastern Publications, 1968. 356 pp.

Yang Hsien-yi, and Yang, Gladys, trs. *Stories About Not Being Afraid of Ghosts.* Peking: Foreign Languages Press, 1961. 89 pp.

TWENTIETH-CENTURY PROSE:

Birch, Cyril, ed. *Chinese Communist Literature.* New York: Praeger Publishers, 1963. 254 pp.

Hsia Tsi-an. *The Gate of Darkness: Studies on the Leftist Literary Movement in China.* Seattle: University of Washington Press, 1968. xxxix, 266 pp. (Paperback).

Hu Shih. *The Chinese Renaissance.* (1934). New York: Paragon Book Gallery, 1964. viii, 110 pp.

Huang, Sung-k'ang. *Lu Hsün and the New Culture Movement of Modern China.* Amsterdam: Djambatan, 1957. 158 pp.

Průšek, Jaroslav, ed. *Studies in Modern Chinese Literature.* Berlin: Akadamie-Verlag, 1964. iv, 179 pp.

Ting Ling [Chiang Ping-chih]. *The Sun Shines Over the Sangkan River.* Tr. by Yang Hsien-yi and Gladys Yang. Peking: Foreign Languages Press, 1954. 348 pp.

Wang Chi-chen, ed. *Stories of China at War.* New York: Columbia University Press, 1947. 158 pp.

GLOSSARY

chih-kuai	Tales of the supernatural—recorded strange events, folk tales and legends.
ching	Classics, *sutras*.
ch'ing-t'an	Pure Discourse—philosophical conversations emphasizing wit.
ch'uan-ch'i	Tales of the marvelous—fiction in the literary language.
fu	Prose-poetry.
hsiao-shuo	"Small talk"—fiction.
hsüan-hsüeh	"Subtle Learning"—Neo-Taoism.
hua-pen	Storyteller's prompt books.
Kuomintang	Nationalist Party, and government of.
ku-wen yen	Literary or classical Chinese.
pai-hua	"Plain speech"—vernacular.
pien-wen	Early vernacular fiction combining poetry with prose.
p'ien-wen	Parallel Prose.
p'ing-hua	Storyteller's tales strung together to form proto-novel.

| shu | History, documents. |
| sutra | Sanskrit for scripture. |

Index

Authors, editors, translators, and titles given in each numbered entry are all presented below in a single alphabetic listing. Please note that the usefulness of this index is limited: persons and titles referred to in the body of the annotations and in the introduction are not indexed. Since this bibliography is arranged chronologically and by topical groupings, the incompleteness of the index, the general editor hopes, is justifiable.